Valiant Living:
Do You Have What It Takes?

by

William "Bill" Blake, Jr., Ph.DRS

Copyright © 2009 by William "Bill" Blake, Jr., Ph.DRS

Valiant Living: Do You Have What It Takes?
by William "Bill" Blake, Jr., Ph.DRS

Printed in the United States of America

ISBN 978-1-60791-637-6

All rights reserved solely by the author. The author guarantees all contents are original and do not infringe upon the legal rights of any other person or work. No part of this book may be reproduced in any form without the permission of the author. The views expressed in this book are not necessarily those of the publisher.

Unless otherwise indicated, Bible quotations are taken from The New King James Version (NKJV) of the Bible, Copyright © 1982 by Thomas Nelson, Inc., Used by permission, and The Amplified ® Bible (AMP), Copyright © 1954, 1958, 1962, 1964, 1965, 1987 by The Lockman Foundation, Used by permission, and The King James Version of the Bible (KJV), and The Holy Bible, New International Version ®, NIV®, Copyright ©1973, 1978, 1984 by International Bible Society, Used by permission of Zondervan, and The Holy Bible, New Living Translation (NLT), Copyright © 1996 by Tyndale House Publishers, Inc., Wheaton, Illinois 60189, Used by permission, and The Living Bible (TLB), Copyright © 1971 by Tyndale House Publishers, Inc., Wheaton, Illinois 60189, Used by permission.

www.xulonpress.com

Valiant Living

*"Through God we will do valiantly, for it is He who
shall tread down our enemies."
Psalm 60:12*

Dedication

Countless times, I sought the gentle wisdom of Davina Blake to help keep my spiritual compass at true north. I have never been disappointed or discouraged. She loves God and actively pursues Him daily. She is my truest friend, wife and a great example of Christian leadership. Davina, thank you!

Contents

Foreword.. **xvii**
Preface... **xix**
Introduction... **xxiii**

Chapter 1- Made To Be Valiant..........................27
    Righteousness 31
    Grace 31
Chapter 2- Created To Worship.........................35
    Sing To the Lord.. 37
    Is God Real To You 38
    Connected Through Brokenness................ 42
    He is Always There 44
    Trust Him 45
    Keep Your Dance 46
    A Chain Reaction 46
    Be Anxious for Nothing 48
    A Place of Rest...50
    How to Find His Rest.................................52
    Lay It Down and Rest 53
    Kept Promises 54
Chapter 3- Appearing with Jesus 57
    I Want to See Him for Myself....................59
    Reasons for Seeking Him...........................61
    Voice of Authority 64

Chapter 4- Get to Higher Grounds 67
   Think Like God 74
   Outer Evidence 75
   Inner Evidence 80
   Committed 81
   Fight for Holiness 85
Chapter 5- Ambassadors for Christ 87
   Wait On Him 90
   His Desire 91
   Soul Winning 93
   The Perfect You 94
   His Thoughts 96
   Your Destiny 100
   Serve With a Loyal Heart 102
   Prioritize 103
   God is Your Source 105
Chapter 6- Love with a Prayerful Heart 107
Chapter 7- Follow Where God Leads 115
   Knowledge and Understanding 120
   Desire the Things of God 122
Chapter 8- Better to Obey 129
   Wait a Minute 134
   Complete Assurance 135
   Press On 136
   Choose to Serve 139
Chapter 9- Disrespect out of Disobedience 141
   The Spirit of Amalek 143
   The Importance of Light 146
   Chapter 10- The Pretender 149
   Instruments of God 153
Chapter 11- We Belong to Jesus 157
   Stay Close Enough to Hear 157
Chapter 12- My Everything, Oh Most High 163
   Glory and Honor 167
   The Big Harvest 168

    From Heaven to Earth 169
    A Present Help.. 171
Chapter 13- His Sacrifice for Us 173
    His Love 177
    Love One Another 179
    Love is Inclusive 180
    He Took Our Place 185
Chapter 14- All Things Work Together 187
    Healing 188
    Favor 190
    Peace 191
Chapter 15- Prosperity 195
    Instructions on Giving... 198
    Instructions on Receiving 199
    What's His Is Mine 200
    Trust God's Economy 203
Chapter 16- Freedom and Restoration 207
    Salvation 210
Chapter 17- Holy Spirit.. 213

Conclusion 217
End Notes... 223

Acknowledgement

First, I thank God the Father, Creator of heaven and earth; God the Son, my Lord and Savior, Jesus Christ; and God the Holy Spirit, Glorifier of the triune Godhead.

I honor my wife and kids for sacrificing a lot out of their lives to allow me uninterrupted moments to complete this work. I can never recover the opportunities lost during this time. Then again, as a family unit, we are one step closer to where God is leading us.

Next, I honor Ron S. Dryden, my spiritual father in Christ, for teaching me how to apply diligence and focus to change my life while showing mercy out of compassion to others.

Subsequently, I honor Casey and Wendy Treat for taking me to the next level of faith and excellence through their devoted teachings followed by opportunities to apply learned Bible knowledge while serving in the House.

I thank the entire Valiant Living Christian Center church family and Xulon press for this opportunity to share this book. Thank you, Sharilyn S. Grayson (sharilynedits.com), for your editorial support. Thank you, Sharon Bletscher and Aileen L. Miles, for your reviews and formation.

Finally, I honor and applaud the prayers and support of all who gave of their time, talent, and resources to accomplish this effort. I ask the Lord to multiply your giving.

Recognition for Bill Blake

"You are a man whose character and integrity are hard to quantify. You have kept every one of your commitments since we met in Frankfurt, Germany in 1991. You are a very trustworthy, remarkable, and genuine individual!"

Gregory M. McLaughlin
Former Deputy Director, Federal Air Marshal Service - U.S. Marine Corps Veteran

"Bill, you are a solid and exceptional man."

John G. Chamberlain
Special Agent in Charge, Federal Air Marshal Service, Boston - U.S. Army Veteran

"You have kept your integrity, and sometimes that's hard in business. Your words of advice were also right on."

Russell E. Mosher
Transportation Security Administration - U.S. Army Special Forces Veteran

"Your leadership style that includes family as an equally important mission was and is still to this day very refreshing."

Brian E. Donaldson
Homeland Security – U.S. Army Veteran

"Thank you for your encouragement and counsel."

William "Bill" Hammer, J.D.
Federal Air Marshal Service - U.S. Marine Corps Veteran (Staff Judge Advocate)

Foreword

"This new book, Valiant Living, by Bill Blake, is meat for the soul for those who are searching for God, those who are just now growing in the Lord, and those who just need a refreshing of who God really is. If you're asking questions about God's will, plan, or purpose, and what your responsibility is in all of that, then this book is specifically for you. It's a thought provoker that will keep you glued to its powerful revelations. I could hardly put it down! It makes you think, and it makes you believe that God really is just who He says He is. Valiant Living could be a textbook for developing Christians, and it could be a resource book for struggling Christians. It is reinforcement for us all. I highly recommend this new work by Pastor Bill Blake. You won't regret it!"

Ron S. Dryden - Pastor/Founder (retired)
Cathedral of Praise World Outreach Center,
Oklahoma City, OK

Preface

I have been saved for over eighteen years, during which I have periodically struggled to know the active purpose of my life. Life and people can offer some tough blows when you are not sure about things. Of all the things about which I was sure, recognizing my leadership call was not one of them. Even though leading and encouraging others came naturally to me, I struggled to see myself as others around me did. Once I identified and accepted my divine assignment, the blur went away, and my focus kindled a deep desire to encourage, lead, and build others up even more. I have always been called to lead others while in the Marine Corps and within the federal government, but I never really made anything of those calls, except that I had a pretty good job with benefits and that I was chosen again to lead.

A few years ago, thoughts of leading others apart from my job really began to look attractive, and they drew me into a deep quest to know what my next assignment would be. I went through a series of projects to challenge me, but none brought fulfillment as I thought they would. On December 14, 2007, I resigned my executive-level position with the Department of Homeland Security to pursue God until I found out what my assignment was. I embarked upon a ravenous feeding of the Word of God and focused prayer. The Lord first gave me the desire to start an organization to help fight homelessness. Afterwards, the desire to write this book consumed me as the words literally poured onto the pages. Recently, God gave me a vision to pioneer a church in a nearby city. After becoming available for God's use and putting aside everything to pursue Him, I have seen Him do marvelous things in my life! The walk has been challenging but very fulfilling.

This book will illustrate and enhance the simplicity of knowing and walking with God. It will also reduce the burden placed on man by commonplace standards. God loves us, as He proved by the sacrificial offering of His one and only begotten Son to purchase our salvation. God, through the person of the Holy Spirit, participated in the immaculate conception of Jesus. We receive His Spirit upon confessing with our mouths and believing in our hearts (Romans 10:9-10). Jesus is the manifest offspring of God's Spirit overshadowing Mary. We receive adoption of the same Spirit through our belief in the works of the cross.

Within the following pages, you will be exposed to some struggles that I took years to recognize and find effective ways to approach. Without exception you will recognize nuggets from the hearts and minds of others in addition to my own. Let me be first to acknowledge their influence upon this work. My father, William Blake, Sr., was a man of deep wisdom, character, and discipline; you will hear his voice repeatedly throughout this work. My mother, Rebecca Blake, poured in me the habit of quickly forgiving myself, others, and to move on with life. It has made all the difference in my life! My seven brothers and sisters all gave me opportunity to practice what my parents taught me. I have benefitted from countless revelations while being taught by others far more superior in Word knowledge than I. My hope is that this book serves to be a timely emphasis under the right conditions to comfort and speak to the needs of the reader.

My sincere desire is that you boldly peel back layers containing hurdles that have held you back from successes you should have accomplished by this season in your life. This kind of spiritual work was hard for me to do, but I found the strength necessary to get it done. Subsequently, I still fight to maintain the ground I have gained. However, I trust that, by making my experiences transparent to you, I can help you to find the needed strength to step out of the shadows of others and things hindering you from enjoying your seasons of accomplishments. I believe you can find that strength lying dormant on the inside of you. I want to show you how God will help you live a valiant life, fulfilling and exceeding your best dreams as you submit and use your God-given talents and abilities to eliminate obstacles that keep you entangled, pressed for time, and void of the needed energy to pursue higher ground. You have my full support as you let go of the former things that took place in your life to allow God to exceed your highest expectations abundantly. He has been longing to awaken your life. Let go, and let God!

Introduction

Have you ever wondered why the most powerful Source known desires a personal relationship with each person, from every walk of life, around the entire world? My explanation for this desire derives from the design of the institution of family. The more and closer family members are, the greater the impact and effect of showing and telling everyone who the family is, of what it consists, and the common purpose driving each member to sustain its very existence.

We have an innate desire to be with others for various reasons. Some seek approval and acceptance, while others yearn for fellowship. We like to fellowship with people and surround ourselves with others. The type of people with whom we fellowship contributes to the course of our lives. People of similar likes and dislikes flock together. We are most comfortable with those who appear to identify with us. Very few people gather with those of opposite interests. Those who do risk relations with others unlike themselves experience the most growth and achieve influence.

God obligates us to fellowship with Him and His people. *"That which we have seen and heard we declare to you, that you also may have fellowship with us; and truly our fellow-*

ship is with the Father and with His Son Jesus Christ" (1 John 1:3). God the Father, God the Son, and God the Holy Spirit are in complete harmony with each other, so much so that we cannot tell where one ends and another begins. One! This unity is a matter of the heart.

The heart of a believer must have and express these seven essentials:

1. Purity (1 Samuel 16:7)
2. Humility (Numbers 12:3)
3. Patience (Genesis 29:20)
4. Consistency (Daniel 3:16-18)
5. Zeal (Acts 8:17-22)
6. Wisdom (Acts 17:16-23)
7. Honesty (Mathew 5:37)

We are to fellowship with one another spiritually while continuing the unfinished ministry of winning souls by lifting high the name of Jesus and glorifying God!

Continuing the ministry of Jesus to win the lost and meet the needs of the world while strengthening the body of Christ is a very high calling. *"Most assuredly, I say to you, he who believes in Me, the works that I do he will do also; and greater works than these he will do, because I go to My Father. And whatever you ask in My name, that I will do, that the Father may be glorified in the Son. If you ask anything in my name, I will do it" (John 14:12-14).*

Each believer must activate and appropriate five key principles in his personal life in order to have influence:

1. Focus on Others (Isaiah 42:16; Galatians 6:2)
2. Focus on Change (Matthew 18:11; James 1:21)
3. Focus on Results (John 17:12)
4. Mentor with Wisdom (Matthew 10:16)
5. Show Compassion (Luke 10:33-36; Matthew 11:28)

God requires these works of valiant believers. I believe that every believer has what he needs to be valiant. Those who are actively doing the works serve as a beacon of hope for those who have yet to discover the bold courage lying dormant inside of them. I pray that this work inspires you to the level of being a courageous soldier for the kingdom of God!

If you are tired of a tedious life going nowhere, make a change. Life will offer many things to you, most of which you can do without. Stress, doubt, and a desire to throw in the towel seem to be the overriding theme of our day. I want to show you how God will help you live a valiant life of fulfillment and success as you submit to God and use the talents and abilities He gave you to eliminate obstacles that keep you entangled, pressed for time, and void of the needed energy to pursue higher ground. You have to match force with force that is equal to or better than your challenges in order to move forward! During the windy seasons of your life, you have to lean forward with force to take your next step. Running life's race requires you to maintain long-term endurance to outpace obstacles. Challenging burdens place a demand on your inner strength to power through opposition explosively. Apply the force on force principle to your personal life, and live valiantly. Fight the good fight!

Father God, I ask that all who read and meditate on the words and principles expressed in this book will be stirred to know and execute courageously, through the gifts you have liberally given each, their callings to their highest potential in order to further the kingdom of God on earth as it is in heaven, in the name of Jesus. Amen!

Chapter 1

Made to Be Valiant

What does being valiant mean? Webster simply defines *valiant* as the quality of being worthy, strong and courageous, acting with a brave boldness to exhibit a focused determination.[1] In today's world, our military stands and fights to uphold freedoms we currently enjoy. However, outside of the armed forces, we MUST dare to fight and win other battles. I'm talking about the battles in our war to maintain holiness.

> *For those who live according to the flesh set their minds on the things of the flesh, but those who live according to the Spirit, the things of the Spirit.*
> Romans 8:5

We have to be valiant in our daily choices to ensure a lifestyle of holiness. I want to be perfectly clear on this point. You determine your level of holiness through the daily choices you make over the course of your life. Holiness does not happen out of thin air. You have to fight for it. Many people would like to see those of us who have chosen to live holy fall in disgrace to prove right their unbelief and life choices contrary to holiness. We must fight many battles all at the same time. We fight to keep our kids in an environment of holiness. We fight to ensure that our youth, who are the future of our country, remain aligned to the beliefs, principles, and way of God. We fight to ensure that the church, the body of Christ, is recognized and not smothered in layers of rules and policy to the point of not being an effective refuge for its members and others who choose to worship God freely. Further, Romans 8:7 explains that *"the carnal mind is enmity against God; for it is not subject to the law of God, nor indeed can be."*

> The Message Bible puts the idea this way:
> *Focusing on the self is the opposite of focusing on God. Anyone completely absorbed in self ignores God, ends up thinking more about self than God. That person ignores who God is and what He is doing. And God isn't pleased at being ignored.*
> *Romans 8:7*

While in the Marine Corps traveling around the world, I thought, for that certain time in my life, that I was my own person who could do as I wanted where I wanted and how I wanted. Out of my empty quest to prove this theory, which I didn't, I was hollow, lonely, and ashamed of everything I did and said and everywhere I went. When you get to the end of you, then you have a unique moment to recognize and meet God, who is the origin and completion of your life. If you allow Him to lead you, you will be a whole lot happier and more successful in life while meeting the spoken and unspoken needs of others around you.

Always remember those of the faith gone on before us who possessed and acted with the bravery and boldness of valor to ensure that the church is alive and well today. Conducting their lives out of obedience with the courage and determination to live a personal experience, they cultivated a deep devoted relationship with God our Creator, possessing His promises, gifts, and passion to love His people. Taking on valiant character or attributes while living out the definition of valor means that you:

- Distinguish who God made you to be.
- Discover what He created you to do.
- Define how you will fulfill His plan for your life.
- Determine to do what He wills.

Psalm 60:12 declares, *"Through God we will do valiantly."* Those of us who dare to put on the armor of God and live valiantly will discover true success and our purpose for living. Following the creative process of the Almighty and eternal God in whom we believe, we understand that God prepared a place of dominion rule for man within the created atmosphere of earth. Upon completing the environment for man to rule, the triune Godhead created and introduced man to his new habitat.

Let Us make man in Our image, according to Our likeness; let them have dominion over the fish of the sea, over the birds of the air, and over every creeping thing that creeps on the earth.
Genesis 2:26

God made man in His likeness. Therefore, man has tendencies similar to his Creator. Within God is perfect courage, worth, and determination. We live drawing from that perfection to become as He is. When God created man in His likeness, the very act communicated a strong desire to relate with His creation. The Bible records God identifying Abraham as His friend (see 2 Chronicles 20:7). Friends are generally people with whom we surround ourselves who both enjoy being with us and have our best interest at heart. To be called a friend of God is most desirable! When God replaced Saul as king, He did so with David, *"a man after His own heart"* (*1 Samuel 13:14*). Daily, God walked through the Garden in the cool of the day to visit and fellowship with Adam and Eve (see Genesis 3:8). He wanted to see man take dominion over His creation through faithful stewardship. Adam failed at the initial dominion given in the Garden. However, God did not dismiss future communion with man. Realizing God's initiative after the fall of Adam, we must ask this question: why does man struggle to develop and maintain a significant relationship with God?

For us to achieve oneness with God through any work of our flesh is impossible. *"Not by power nor by might, but by My Spirit"* (*Zachariah 4:6*). Jesus made a way for us through the shedding of His holy innocent blood by way of the cross. While the change in man was not outwardly visible immediately after Jesus' sacrifice, He instantly established a direct spiritual connection to God. Man's spirit immediately regained synchronization with that of the Father. Man can now receive, through his spirit, direct wisdom, understanding, and revelation knowledge from God. Stop trying so hard within your humanness to qualify for God's righteousness and grace. All you have to do is believe, receive, and walk in that grace as if you already have it, and it will become an automatic way of life for you.

We find this confirmation in the Message Bible, which says:

> *Are you tired? Worn out? Burned out on religion? Come to me. Get away with me and you'll recover your life. I'll show you how to take a real rest. Walk with me and work with me – watch how I do it. Learn the unforced rhythms of grace.*
>
> *Matthew 11:28-29*

Righteousness

Righteousness is the quality or condition of being morally sound or just. Sincerity and humility are key attributes of a righteous person. Scripture teaches that *"treasures of wickedness profit nothing, but righteousness delivers from death (Proverbs 10:2)*. This verse suggests that righteousness can be staged for effect with man, but not with God, because He sees the true intention of the heart (Hebrews 4:12). Many people live their lives outside of God's righteousness. Many have died to inherit eternal separation from God for not knowing and observing righteousness. Righteousness is measured by God's standard and not man's. The righteousness of God in the life of a believer acts like a canopy to cover and shelter the believer from negative influences found in the world. Let me say what I mean this way: the old life and character that you had prior to confessing Jesus as Lord had very little spiritual influence for the kingdom of God. That life had to be codified and, yes, eradicated unto death (2 Corinthians 5:17). The righteousness of God covers, hides, and over time erases any impact your past could have on your new life in Him. Subsequently, the righteousness of God has hidden your past through the works Jesus Christ accomplished on the cross of Calvary! Because righteousness is the standard of God, you must purpose to maintain righteousness in your life. You did not earn righteousness; God gave it to you as a free gift through His grace.

Grace

We do not win the fight of living according to God's righteousness on the battlefield of life. That victory happens in the mind. *"Set your mind on the things above, not on the things of the earth. For you died, and your life is hidden with Christ in God" (Colossians 3:2-3)*. The very moment you possess an unwavering belief in the success of the mission Jesus accomplished through the work of the cross to paralyze, eradicate, and disconnect believers from sin and shame, you win the battle for righteousness! Now act like you won! Walk out the triumph! If you walk it out, then Jesus will work it out on your behalf!

Grace is the free, unmerited love and favor of God. It is the influence of divinity acting in man to restrain him from sin. Grace is a state of reconciliation to God. Inside grace, God supplies us with spiritual instruction, improvement, and edification towards righteousness. As I read and understand the Bible, I see no indication that the receiver (man) earned such a state as grace or influenced the Giver (God) to bestow it on him. *"For by grace you have been saved through faith, and that not of yourselves; it is the gift of God, not of works, lest anyone should boast"* (Ephesians 2:8.) The same truth is unequivocally clear in Romans 4:4, *"Now to him who works, the wages are not counted as grace but as debt."* You can't earn grace! It's a gift from God for us to accept or reject.

The mail handler who delivers your mail is responsible for collecting, sorting, and delivering parcels addressed to you. The handler's job is not to ensure that you are acquainted with or take notice of the content. Once he delivers the parcel to your box, his job is done. You have the onus to open your box and receive your mail or reject it. Well, God has filled your box with grace and righteousness, personally ensuring the delivery through the precious life blood of Jesus. Open your box and receive! All is of grace and grace is for all.

Again, you cannot earn grace or righteousness. However, you can obtain them by *faith* when you believe in the finished work of the cross. Prior to leaving heaven, Jesus decided that the victory had been won. The mission was worth dying for. All He had to do was to execute and complete the mission. His crucifixion on that wooden cross bore the curse of sin: *"Christ has redeemed us from the curse of the law, having become a curse for us (For it is written, "Cursed is everyone who hangs on a tree") (Galatians 3:13)*. He took the curse of death for our sins. His death and burial marked the end of the law and the beginning of faith justification freeing us from the condemnation of sin, shame, and death: *"For Christ is the end of the law for righteousness to everyone who believes" (Romans 10:4)*. The evil one uses the shame of sin to keep us bound, shackled, and ineffective for God. Not wanting the shame of our sin exposed to others quiets us. As a believer in the events leading up to Calvary and beyond, you have to know for yourself that your debt for sin and shame – past, present and future — has been paid in full! Do not abuse, make light, or neglect the grace that has been extended to you. *"For as by one man's disobedience many were made sinners, so also by one Man's obedience many will be made righteous" (Romans 5:19)*.

> Jesus paid it all,
> All to Him I owe.
> Sin had left a Crimson stain;
> He washed it [me] white as snow.
> Elvina M. Hall[2]

His resurrection and ascension established life eternal for all humanity: *"I am the resurrection and the life. He who believes in Me, though he may die, he shall live" (John 11:25)*. Jesus prophetically said these words to Martha at Lazarus' gravesite. Jesus had not died yet, but He believed in the victory of His mission and acted on its power to establish the kingdom of God before those many observers at the gravesite. What He did then, He will do again.

> *For the Lord Himself will descend from heaven with a shout, with the voice of an archangel, and with the trumpet of God. And the dead in Christ will rise first.*

Then we who are alive and remain shall be caught up together to meet the Lord in the air. And thus we shall always be with the Lord. Therefore comfort one another with these words.
1 Thessalonians 4:16–18

After God raised Jesus through the power of the Holy Spirit, Jesus ascended into heaven, and He is presently seated at the right hand of the Father where He initially started. He will return to fulfill Scripture! I believe that we who are saved will be with the Lord as Scripture promises. I look forward to the day of this occurrence. However, what happens until then? We are to live valiantly advancing the kingdom of God! When our time here is over, we will access eternity and experience Jesus as He is in fullness. The complete glory of God will be revealed to us! Moses saw a shadow of what we will see in full when Jesus returns. The reward for living by faith and finishing our race will be to appear with Jesus. *"Eye has not seen, nor ear heard, nor have entered into the heart of man the things which God has prepared for those who love Him" (1 Corinthians 2:9).* We will greatly admire His divine presence.

> You are beautiful beyond description,
> Too marvelous for words,
> Too wonderful for comprehension,
> Like nothing ever seen or heard.
> Who can grasp your infinite wisdom?
> Who can fathom the depths of your love?
> You are beautiful beyond description,
> Majesty enthroned above.
>
> Mark Altrogge[3]

Chapter 2

Created to Worship
A Mighty Fortress

Worship is a continual expression of our deepest gratitude for everything God has done, is doing, and will do for us!

> *Bless the Lord, O my soul; and all that is within me, bless His holy name! Bless the Lord, O my soul and forget not all His benefits; who forgives all your iniquities, who heals all your diseases.*
>
> Psalm 103:1-3

The Bible instructs us to worship God always. *"Praise God in His sanctuary; praise Him in His mighty firmament! Let everything that has breath praise the Lord. Praise the Lord!" (Psalm 150:1, 6).* Worship is the means by which we experience God's glory and the beauty of His presence, bringing healing, unspeakable joy, and restoration to every area of our being. David said, *"You will show me the path of life; in Your presence is fullness of joy; at Your right hand are pleasures forevermore"* (Psalm 16:11).

God is a God of praise. Because He is God, He is worthy of our praise and adoration. Psalm 96:4 states, *"For the Lord is great and greatly to be praised; He is to be feared [respected and reverenced] above all gods."* God has specifically reserved His right to be collectively and universally praised for His supreme rule. As expressed in Isaiah 42:8, *"I am the Lord, that is My name; and My glory I will not give to another. Nor My praise to carved images."* God expressed His own unique vulnerability, as we understand the term, through jealousy over our praise of Him only.

You shall not make for yourself a carved image – any likeness of anything that is in heaven above, or that is in the earth beneath, or that is in the water under the earth; you shall not bow down to them. For I, the Lord your God, am a jealous God.
Exodus 20:4-5

Carved images are lifeless, dead, and nonresponsive. God is alive. He is the only one and true living God of all.

If you accept the fact that God is the only one and true living God, you must go further to understand that He has the vision of eyes to see, the reception of ears to hear, the faculty of thought to think, the mechanics of hands to touch, the oration of speech to talk, and the insight and sensitivity of passion to feel. God is so careful in His description of carved images that He leaves us with just one viable option. Either we worship gods carved from the vain imagination of man to no avail, or we worship the living Creator of the universe. If you spend more time polishing and tuning your car than you do worshiping God, then you have created an idol. If you perfect the growth of vegetables and rose bushes in your garden and negate your personal growth with the Lord, then you have created an idol. If your fascination and fixation on your cell phone and the Internet are your best friends, keeping you away from quality time with God, then you have created an idol. If your thoughts of infatuation continuously focus on any one person more than God, then you have created an idol. We must keep a balance in life for all things. I choose to worship the one and true *living* God of all while freely enjoying all things.

In John's vision, the four beasts described in the book of Revelation 4:8 endlessly worshiped God with praise, saying, *"Holy, holy, holy, Lord God Almighty, Who was and is and is to come!"* I believe that the very fuel of their continual worship of the Almighty was endless revelation. Each time they would straighten from bowing to behold the indescribable beauty of God, the vision vehemently compelled them to pour out *"Holy, holy, holy."* Although they were designed to praise God at His throne, they were exposed to deeper and deeper revelations that left them overwhelmed. God is so glorious that the very sight of His person overpowered the spiritual, creative existence of the four, leaving them speechless to describe their Maker. Actually, God was praising Himself through the creative existence of the four. We should not wonder if we are left overwhelmed in the presence of God through high worship and praise.

Further, the twenty-four elders said, *"You are worthy, O Lord, to receive glory and honor and power; for You created all things, and by Your will they exist and were created" (Revelation 4:10-11).* In other words, without God, we have no life. He brings life to our very existence. *"For in Him we live, and move, and have our being" (Acts 17:28).*

Sing to the Lord

I have learned to keep hymns and songs of praise all around me. I love praise and worship music and the element it adds to the atmosphere of worship. A worship song is one that has lyrics which help you focus on loving God, Jesus Christ, and the sweet presence of the Holy Spirit. Accordingly, the spirit of the song could have the exact same influence. A worship song with lyrics to help paint a picture of what you can't express in words but sense intrinsically will always demand participation from a true worshiper.

Rejoice in the Lord, O you righteous! For praise from the upright is beautiful. Praise the Lord with the harp; make melody to Him with ten strings. Sing to Him a new song; play skillfully with a shout of joy.
Psalm 33:1–3

God is very pleased when we worship Him with songs of praise and musical instruments. Likewise, God loves the unique sound of our individual voices. Do not bypass an opportunity to praise Him with your voice! Have you ever sung a personal song from your heart to God? It may not be a best-seller on the music charts, but God loves it nonetheless! When you are in His presence, the communication from your heart is very important to God. Singing praise and worship creates an atmosphere that brings the presence of God.

Is God Real to You?

I recall the very first time I experienced God's presence. I had just joined the Cathedral of Praise, World Outreach Center (COPWOC) in Oklahoma City where Ron S. Dryden, my spiritual father, was founder and senior pastor. This church was big, by my guess two hundred and sixty-four thousand square feet with seating capacity for five thousand members. Mind you, growing up I attended a very small Methodist church (twenty-one hundred square feet with parking included), mostly family members, in Red Top, South Carolina. My experience at COPWOC was such a big transition for me because I had only seen facilities like it on TV like *The 700 Club, TBN,* etc.

After becoming a member, I volunteered for everything. One of my volunteer places was temple ministry; I thought that the ministry would be like what Aaron the priest did. At the time, making sacrificial offerings appealed to me. I had not been saved long during this time, and I found myself one of few members who consistently showed up to fulfill my commitment. After a lonely season of this service, I would have liked to offer up some as a sacrifice. While serving in this ministry, I realized a slight difference between Aaron's offering and mine. I became one of the actual sacrifices offered. I gave countless hours weekly to clean the church buildings and grounds. I gave my time, labor, and resources as a sacrifice to God through this ministry.

The church owned a titanic commercial vacuum cleaner nicknamed "Big Bertha." On this particular day, she and I started dancing and singing. One thing led to another, and I found myself in the presence of God, worshiping! I was shaking visibly and internally while crying out of control. Big Bertha must have filled this exact purpose previously, because she was so good in providing me cover from any potential embarrassment as I tearfully cried aloud. She just sat there patiently running, waiting on me to start again.

At the time, I was the only one in the sanctuary, but I was still uneasy with the experience of exposing my vulnerability in a public place. The twelve by eight feet glass panel sliding doors that gave access into the sanctuary soundproofed my encounter from those walking by who paid me no attention. That relative privacy was a good thing, because I was not comfortable emotionally expressing myself in public. I thought that any emotional display of this kind was a sign of weakness. I have since gotten over my stubborn stronghold of resisting God in public. Perhaps, as God has matured me in my walk with Him, these encounters have made Him irresistible to me. He continues to draw me near. In the midst of my unfaithfulness, He is always faithful. In the midst of my trials, He is my strong tower, a shelter from every storm. For me, to be with Him in private and dishonor Him in public by disassociation is inappropriate. My current stay is: *"Thy will be done" (Matthew 6:10, KJV)*.

After personally experiencing the overwhelming presence of God, I agree with A.W. Tozer, who said, *"I want the presence of God Himself or I don't want anything at all to do with religion...I want all that God has or I don't want any."*[4]

I recall another afternoon in prayer, sitting on the floor of my bedroom. I was somewhat low in spirit because I did not understand this new level of being with God. People were speaking and singing in their prayer languages and testifying of great things happening in their lives. Although I was out serving most others around me as a new member, I did not have a prayer language, and I was slightly discouraged. I was beginning to think that I should throw in the towel. I had no joy, just extreme fatigue from serving.

Well, the Lord visited me, and I began to laugh aloud for no reason. I could not stop, and the intensity became so strong that my laughter came up from my shaking stomach, the kind that makes the lower back of your head ache! I began to cry and laugh and cry and laugh. I was concerned, because I had seen others this way on occasions for no apparent reason. In retrospect, I saw clearly that the Holy Spirit was working. I could not stop! After about thirty minutes, the laughing slowed to a steady chuckle with occasional outburst of laughter. When the experience was all over, I realized what others were talking about when they testified of God's presence and goodness. David insisted in Psalm 34:8, *"Oh, taste and see that the Lord is good."* Once you experience His presence, you remain hungry for more of the same!

God visited and ministered to my spirit of discouragement until I recovered. I did not verbally ask for joy. He gave it to me because He understood what I could not say with words because of my heaviness. Just like a playful parent, He tickled me into laughter which replaced my burden with His joy! Just worship Him, because He knows all about you. During your worship, He will do the rest! Don't be ashamed of the intimate presence of God.

From time to time, I see what appears to be a couple walking. The woman is emotionally transparent, and she cannot hide the fact that she has been intimate with the man who is walking slightly ahead or behind her as if they were not together. She desires to be seen with him in public to make the statement, "We are given to each other." However, he wants to farm around, and so he plays it safe by staying close enough for her to have a sense of belonging but far enough for others to wonder. If he is pleased to be with her in private, he should honor her in public. He should shout at the top of his lungs: "She is mine, and I am hers, and God be with anyone who attempts to divide us!"

We tend to treat God the same way. Some say, "I will praise You when no one is looking. I'll sing and dance in the privacy and comfort of my home. I will pray, read the Bible, and pray in the spirit, but do not ask me to do so in public. Overshadow me at home, in my car, or in the shower where I can really sing out loud, but not where others will see me or challenge my relationship with You." Well, this relationship is not about us. We were created to make His name glorious. *"Sing out the honor of His name; make His praise glorious" (Psalms 66:2)*. The thing that you love the most will always be the focus of your conversation and drive your daily actions. Others will know you by your words and actions. Are you representing holiness? Do others know you to be a believer? Does your life bring awareness and glory to God? These qualities too, are forms of worship.

The presence of God is always with me. I cherish it so much that I fight spiritually, mentally, and physically to maintain an atmosphere which is inviting to Him. My maturity and growth in God has increased since honoring His presence. He is with me at all times, especially when I am serving others. I have come to a place in my life where the most important thing to me, bar none, is the presence of God. *"The grass withers, the flower fades, but the word of God stands forever" (Isaiah 40:8).* I have had many seasons in my life to date. Some of them were good and some not so good. The single most constant and unchanging element that sustained me through them all was the eminent presence of God!

Connected through Brokenness

From age twelve until thirty-two or thereabouts, no one had ever seen me shed tears. I played college football, served eight years in the United States Marine Corps, and completed a full career in Law Enforcement; so my bearing was hardened even the more. I could always control my emotions. I had been told by my dad, "Men don't cry!" He later changed and took back this statement, relieving me of that heartless burden which has made the difference in my life. My opinion is that for a man to cry out to God, who can and will deliver him, is an act of good judgment. At about the age of thirty-three, I had a unique visitation from the Lord. I did not really know that such a visitation could actually happen outside the pages of the Bible. My shallow understanding of the Holy Spirit argued with a gentle visit, let alone His effective administration to bring healing and restoration. I customarily prayed for a visitation with unbelief, because I was in the middle of everyone else praying for the same and felt obligated to do so. I appeared to fit in with the crowd, but I never believed God would favor me especially.

The Holy Spirit was a completely different concept to me growing up. I always thought that the Holy Spirit was present when someone was screaming and jumping out of control, causing two or more church members to hold them down, temporarily delaying the service. Much to my surprise, as the Holy Spirit ministered to me, I did shake and cry. My not having to be restrained, screaming, or delaying the service was not a disappointment to me. I later understood that the Holy Spirit is a person, in reality, who knows how to pay an effective, cordial visit. Whenever He senses a reverent invitation inside an atmosphere of holiness, the Spirit of God will always manifest Himself.

Now I know that the Holy Spirit represents God's presence since the ascension of Jesus. Some may argue that today we are without direct access to Jesus like the twelve disciples had with Him. They visibly saw and physically touched Him while hearing His voice. For these disciples, a level of faith was required. As we read the Bible, through faith, we have the exact same exposure to our Lord. However, a higher level of faith is required because we cannot visibly see or physically touch Him. *"The word which they heard did not profit them, not being mixed with faith in those who heard it" (Hebrews 4:2).* We should cling to the truth and principles in the Bible more today than at any other time in the history of humanity. We today have the exact same access to the Lord by faith. *"Jesus Christ is the same yesterday, today, and forever" (Hebrews 13:8).* Our life opens and closes with the divine. *"Jesus, the author and finisher of our faith" (Hebrews 12:2).* Our direct access to the supernatural is a matter of mind and soul over body. *"If you can believe, all things are possible to Him who believes" (Mark 9:23).*

Right now, lift your hands and let God know how much He means to you. Give Him glory for His endless faithfulness to you!

How can I say thanks for the things You have done for me?
Things so undeserved, yet You gave to prove Your love for me.
Voices of a million angels could not express my gratitude!
All that I am and ever hope to be, I owe it all to You.
To God be the glory for the things He has done!

Vickie Winans[5]

He Is Always There

When you first come to know God in your spirit, you may think that swimming in joy is the standard for your daily life. You think that you are the only one with this experience. While this condition is most desirable, it is not the norm. Yes, this condition is the exact same illumination from the Almighty that many in biblical history encountered of God during their personal visitations. The Father has extended this special consideration to show a peek into His glorious being to those who are His. If He kept you there, two things would happen. Your physical body would shut down from His preeminence, and you would not fully develop into a soldier hardened for spiritual battle.

While in His presence, your *"joy is unspeakable and full of the Glory of God" (1 Peter 1:8)*. You do no wrong, say no wrong, and think no wrong. While working out your salvation, you may feel at times that God is far away. If you are not careful during this time to discern God's love for you, you will misinterpret the purpose of His presence. You begin to think that you did something wrong because you cannot feel His presence. Never forget that God is omnipresent. Wherever you are, He was, is, and will be again. He will never leave you. *"Lo, I am with you always, even to the end of the age" (Matthew 28:20).* He is always with you! You need to know this truth and press on.

Trust Him

Do you trust the will of God? Because His will is His prerogative, He sets the schedule and time for all events perfecting His will in our lives. Job understood the inconsistency of trusting in others when he said, *"Man who is born of woman is of few days and full of trouble" (Job 14:1).* Being born of the flesh brings inevitable turmoil that limits our ability to function as God intended. Without relationship of trust and the presence of God in our lives, we will surely self-destruct.

The presence of God visited Mary to solicit her participation in a cornerstone event that shaped Christianity. After a time of conversation with the angel, Mary understood the basics of what would come from her immaculate conception. She worshiped by saying, *"Behold the maidservant of the Lord! Let it be to me according to your word" (Luke 1:38).* Now, imagine having this level of excitement about such an event. If you are not careful, you could share your news with someone who does not understand or is not concerned with the matter. The wrong person speaking into your life in a vulnerable and critical season of transition could sabotage a faith opportunity from God. Mary kept her conversation limited to Elizabeth, her cousin, who also was expecting a miracle birth. I will give you this piece of advice: if you feel the need to talk, keep your conversation in the family of like faith members. Anyone else will talk you out of your faith moment. Mary kept her trust in the sent Word of God and made history that influences the world to this day and forever because of her ready trust in the will of God.

Keep Your Dance

As you walk with God, you will find yourself in challenges that seem to present no possible way out. Consider with whom you are walking. Focus on His ability, not your ability, your current circumstance, or the ability of the enemy. While others moan and complain, keep your joyful dance of worship before God, and He will deliver you. Job 14:14 asks and answers, *"If a man dies, shall he live again? All the days of my hard service I will wait, till my change comes."* While his trusted friends visited him, he could have allowed himself to sink into the awkward counsel they gave. Nonetheless, Job decided to remind himself of his personal relationship with God, and he surrendered his future to God's intensive care. He stirred himself in worship to the Lord and recovered his joy and possessions to the double of all that he previously had. By just worshiping and magnifying God, Job saw God's domain on earth become like that of the heavens.

> Lift high the Lord our banner,
> Lift high the Lord Jesus King.
> Lift high the Lord our banner,
> Lift high your praise to Him, sing.
>
> For He is wonderful,
> For He reigns on high.
> For He is marvelous,
> The Lord draweth nigh.

Fletch Wiley[6]

A Chain Reaction

Most of us have probably received a chain letter at some point in our lives. A chain letter is a short message typed or hand-written which closes with instructions to copy the letter numerous times and send it to multiple friends. Now, usually the message carries a warning of impending tragedy if the letters are not copied and redistributed. Fearful of not following the directions of the letter, many reproduce them and send them on their way to others as instructed. One chain letter is estimated to have reached a million people in just two months' time, each carrying the same simple message. This example shows the effectiveness of this principle.

The principle of chaining started many of the business systems we enjoy today. Hundreds of businesses have launched using the concept of employing a few people to recruit a few more, eventually exposing the entire nation to their products or services. A few people could sell products to the world if they could only enlist a few more to help them spread the word. Now, that scenario is what you call a chaining concept.

Well, Jesus, while making His ascension into heaven, challenged His disciples to witness for Him by spreading the news throughout the world: the Good News of the gospel that He arose from the dead and that salvation is available to all who believe. Subsequently, Paul and John wrote letters to witness the power of the Spirit of God. The intent of the letters was to allow the broadest distribution of the gospel until the entire world knew Christ through the witness of the church.

As Christians, we must join the chain of witnesses that continue to worship our Lord and tell the world the Good News of the gospel, whether we write it, speak it, sing it, or live it. We must tell the world that Jesus is alive with one voice! Alert the people of Ephesus that their eventful and busy schedule will end in waste without the Good News. Tell those of Smyrna that even in their poverty, they can be prosperous through the gospel. Inform others from Pergamos that they have a higher life option than that which they live. Tell the people of Thyatira that they are following a dead end route. Advise those at Sardis that their accomplishments are preventing them from going to the next level of success. Encourage those of Philadelphia to press on in their fatigue because they are too close to turn around. Finally, we have to tell those of Laodicea that indecisiveness is not a decision; they have to decide now.

The letters written to the seven churches were distinct messages that must be told to the world. If one Christian tells seven friends that Jesus is the Lily of the valley, then he would multiply by seven. Then encourage those seven to tell seven others that He is the Bright and Morning Star, and the number grows to forty-nine. If each of the forty-nine tells seven others that He is the Fairest of all, the total rises to three hundred and forty-three! Moving on, the three hundred and forty-three will each tell seven more that He is Water to a thirsty land, equaling two thousand four hundred and one. If each of the two thousand four hundred and one tells seven friends that He is a Bridge over troubled waters, the number grows to sixteen thousand eight hundred and seven. Keeping momentum, the sixteen thousand eight hundred and seven tell seven additional new acquaintances that He is King of kings, and we now have one hundred seventeen thousand six hundred and forty-nine armed with the gospel. Now if the one hundred seventeen thousand six hundred and forty-nine each witness to seven others that He is Lord of lords, our impact is eight hundred twenty-three thousand five hundred and forty-three. Finally, if the eight hundred twenty-three thousand five hundred and forty-three each tell seven more that He is an Almighty God, then five million seven hundred sixty-four thousand eight hundred and one will have heard the gospel in a very short order of time! We can spread the gospel throughout the whole world in unity if we each simply commit to sharing our personal testimony of Jesus with seven new people on a regular basis.

Just by increase, the numbers indicate the influence and effectiveness one courageous Christian can have among others. My question to you is: does your life carry the influence required to generate this kind of impact? Are you committed to God in boldness? Can you look others in the face and persuade them through your presence to participate in sharing the Good News? The influence of your conversation and actions will cause others to know you for who you really are.

Be Anxious for Nothing

Philippians 4:6 warns us to *"be anxious for nothing, but in everything by prayer and supplication, with thanksgiving, let your requests be made known to God."* We are living in a most restless age. At one time, people were content to go for a slow ride in a buggy. Then the automobile came, which made fifteen miles per hour intolerable. Now, we ride fifty-five miles per hour and think nothing of it. Certainly, a jet plane riding five hundred nautical miles per hour provides the swiftest and most comfortable mode of transportation. Ironically, incidents of rage on the highways and in the air are at an all-time high.

At one time, people would wait a week for the next train, but now we growl when we miss one section of a revolving door or an elevator. At one time, we would visit our relatives, and we were glad to spend time with them: a full day or even a week. Now, we do well to spend one productive hour with a single member of our immediate family on a daily basis. The world is full of unrest, strife, and challenges. Our pending and declining economy will add no comfort to many who live outside the provisions of God. We need to quiet ourselves and listen to the One who said, *"Come to Me, all you who labor and are heavy laden, and I will give you rest" (Matthew 11:28).*

The deprived live from hand to mouth daily in lack. They need rest. The affluent go to the mountains in the summer and go south in the winter. They need rest. The middle class toil at the same old grinding job for twenty years or better. They need rest. In many homes, both parents work, causing them to shift the children from place to place. The children need rest. Many pursue empty promises of riches, fame, and pleasure. They need rest.

David said in unrest, *"Oh that I had wings like a dove! I would fly away and be at rest" (Psalm 55:6)*. How he captured so well what our hearts feel during challenging opportunities in our lives! We just want to get away from it all. We want an escape. Many are looking to people, places, and things to equate the rest promised by our Lord in the Scripture. I say to these weary ones: no one is like the Lord. No adequate substitute exists. You have perhaps seen this bumper sticker: "Know Jesus, Know Peace [rest] – No Jesus, No Peace!" How true that statement is!

A Place of Rest

I love Matthew 11:28 because it solved a lot of problems for me in my late twenties. A dire need to find direction in my life pressed upon me, and I began to study Scriptures like, *"The Lord is my shepherd, I shall not want" (Psalm 23:1),* which brought me peace as I looked to the Lord who delivered me. After losing my father several years ago, I experienced the deepest sorrow I had ever known. The only thing that comforted me was the reassuring truth of Matthew 11:28; those words comforted my heart.

Sometimes the whole world seemed to be against me; my way was hard and rough. I had reached rock bottom, and I shared my room with a loneliness that almost seemed comforting because I had stayed in this state for months. Even in this depression, I sensed a presence of God and a heart impression saying, *"He will not forsake [me] you nor destroy you, nor forget the covenant of your fathers which He swore to them" (Deuteronomy 4:31)*. That anchor encouraged my heart to find true peace. As I pressed through by listening to praise and worship music, the Spirit of God reminded me that *"all that the Father gives Me will come to Me, and the one who comes to Me I will by no means cast out" (John 6:37)*. As I worshipped the Lord, I drew enough strength to receive His forgiveness for my sin, making me complete in Him again. The joy and peace I experienced have kept me in relationship with Him all these years.

So my favorite, most pivotal Scripture is Matthew 11:28. Jesus looked upon the multitude one day and saw their lives filled with trouble and distress. He opened wide His arms and said, *"Come to Me, all you who labor and are heavy laden, and I will give you rest."* Still today, He calls us into His rest in the same way. Oh, how often we run to His rest in worship and prayer. What sweet comfort and rest we have found in the words of Jesus!

At one time, we would go to church and never be in a hurry for service to end. The songs would last for one hour, and then someone would pray until the my dad started his sermon, which would last for one hour. The people took all of that time and came back at night for more. Now, because of restlessness, if a service is longer than one hour and thirty minutes from parking to leaving, attendance suffers at most churches.

I am not advocating all-day church services, even though they would go far to address most woes of our time. We owe God corporate worship. God is watching His creation with a very careful eye. Psalm 33:18 says, *"The eye of the Lord is on those who fear Him."* We are to respect and reverence Him in worship continually. *"For the eyes of the Lord run to and fro throughout the whole earth, to show Himself strong on behalf of those whose heart is loyal to Him" (2 Chronicles*

16:9). God says, "Do I have a people today who consistently honor and revere My presence so that I can reveal Myself to them in order to draw the world into relationship with Me?" Let's rest in the One who gave us all!

> I'll stand with arms high and heart abandoned
> In awe of the One who gave it all.
> My soul to You, Lord, I surrender; all I have is Yours.
>
> Joel Houston[7]

How to Find His Rest

Finding God's rest is simple. Jesus instructs us to find Him first. Notice that He did not tell us to come to a church building or your friend. Although both have their purposes, first we must come to Christ. Imagine a man who has sinned the night away. In the morning, his conscience is burning him, and he goes to the church seeking rest for his troubled soul. He goes to a little cabinet and talks to another man through a dark cloth. He confesses his misgivings to this man and professes certain words. He leaves the church, but his heart is still heavy. If he would give God time for worship, he would find rest.

Worship is the foundation for rest. As we worship the Lord, we join in the continual praise sessions taking place in the heavens. While participating, we know that our worries and troubles dissolve. Worship removes us from the circumstances that are stripping our rest in Jesus away from us. It also strengthens us to do battle in the middle of our circumstances. Worship gives us rest and refreshes our inner strength to continue the fight for the kingdom.

One day Jesus stopped by a well in a city of Samaria called Sychar. A woman came out to draw water. Jesus talked to her, and soon she was expressing the age-old longing for rest, forgiveness, and peace of mind. He assured her that He could provide everything she needed. He said, *"If you knew the gift of God, and who it is who says to you, 'Give Me a drink,' you would have asked Him, and He would have given you living water" (John 4:10).* The woman was obviously too buried in her troubles to recognize Jesus. Her troubled mind tried to steer the conversation to her family history back to Jacob. Jesus focused the conversation by saying,

> *Whoever drinks of this water will thirst again, but whoever drinks of the water that I shall give him will never thirst. But the water that I shall give him will become a fountain of water springing up into everlasting life.*
>
> *John 4:13-14*

She believed Him and received complete forgiveness for trusting Him. The Bible records her running back into the village on happy feet because she had found in Jesus a place of rest and peace from her troubles. Perhaps you have tried various wells from the world, and they have not satisfied your thirst. I invite you to try Jesus. He will surely satisfy your longing heart. Rest in Jesus.

Lay It Down and Rest

Sometimes I just wanted to throw in the towel and do what everyone else was doing, but I began to rest in the Lord through worship, pulling myself out of despair into the favor of God (FOG) to press on. Do not let circumstances take you out of your resting place in Jesus. Just to maintain your resting place in Him really is a fierce fight sometimes. One day, Peter looked at the traces of his life and wondered if he had done the right thing by following Jesus. This reevaluation came after the rich man refused to do what the other disciples did to follow Jesus. So his pressing thoughts pushed him to remind Jesus saying, *"Lord, See, we have left all and followed you" (Luke 19:27).* Jesus answered and said,

> *And everyone who has left houses or brothers or sisters or father or mother or wife or children or lands, for My name's sake, shall receive a hundredfold, and inherit eternal life.*
>
> Matthew 19:29

In other words, rest easy because you will gain in abundance everything you sacrifice to advance the kingdom of God.

Peter, like many of us, needed to remember why he committed to Christ. In other words, what will be our reward? We are fortunate that the Lord had this answer all clear in His head, because He was able to refocus Peter's wondering mind. In Luke 18:29-30 He said again,

> *Assuredly, I say to you, there is no one who has left house or parents or brothers or wife or children, for the sake of the kingdom of God, who shall not receive many times more in this present time, and in the age to come eternal life.*

This explanation held Peter's focus for the next three and a half chapters.

Kept Promises

You know that Jesus made a number of promises to us when He was here. He promised to send the Holy Spirit, and now the Holy Spirit indwells us. He promised to answer our prayers, and every day His ears remain alert to our every cry. He promised to give us rest for our weary souls. As far as I know and as best I can tell, He kept every single one of His promises!

Growing up, I had always been known for being a very strong and healthy person. At thirteen, I was a risk taker who was willing to try just about anything. Each successful attempt at accomplishing something new gave me an amazing sense of inner strength and confidence. One day my father and three brothers were out getting firewood, and I focused on a forty-five inch diameter by three feet long hickory log that my dad's twenty-four inch chainsaw had just cut. I was determined to lift the log onto the tailgate of our transport trailer, which was about three feet from the ground. I patiently rolled the log to the tailgate and stood it up on end to lift it into the trailer. Now the time had come to face my challenge. As I got one end of the log onto the tailgate of the trailer, I realized that the weight was more than I could handle. I called for my dad as the log hit the ground. And not missing a beat, he helped me lift the log, insisting that I put the bulk of the weight on him. Perhaps I didn't realize the significance then, but in that moment, he taught me the value of being able to call on someone for help. Listen, we have many burdens to tolerate in life. We cannot carry them all by ourselves. Nevertheless, if we call on Jesus, He will carry our burdens and us, too. Cast your cares on Him, and let His mighty hands carry you to a place of rest!

Over two thousand years ago, Jesus directly addressed a weary crowd, saying, *"Come to Me, all you who labor and are heavy laden, and I will give you rest" (Matthew 11:28).* He is still saying those words today. Bring everything to Him, because He can bear it. If you do, I promise that His undying love and mercy will illuminate your soul. Worship the Lord Jesus, and praise His holy name. David declared, *"This is my resting place forever; here I will dwell for I have desired it" (Psalm 132:14).* Worship is a place of rest. Get there!

Chapter 3

Appearing with Jesus
Lover of My Soul

~~~

We have to live carefully and manage ourselves through the many challenges life offers. We who believe in Jesus are not on this journey alone. He has granted us unlimited and immediate access to Him and His entire corporation of heavenly resources. Our Lord has done everything possible to ensure us victory in this life on earth. We must pursue by faith fully assured deep in our hearts that Jesus has both given us the victory and made a way for it to come to pass. Scripture identifies Him as our greatest supporter. 1 John 2:1 says that *"we have an Advocate with the Father, Jesus Christ the righteous."* In other words, Jesus has a legitimate right to go before the Father while representing us. Through our faith in His righteousness, we have access to the same throne room with Him. His relationship with the Father is so close that He gained us the same access utilizing His credentials. How precious is the name of Jesus!

Jesus has dedicated His eternal existence to keeping us before the Father in prayer.

But He, because He continues forever, has an unchangeable priesthood. Therefore He is able to save to the uttermost those who come to God through Him, since He always lives to make intercession for them.
Hebrews 7:24-25

God has everything that we need, and He has already made it available to us. Our part is to thank Him for giving us what we need and to receive it by faith.

I've learned through the years that, just as I had the same expectation of help from my earthly dad at thirteen, our heavenly Father desires to see this same expectation in us for Him and His promises. *"Let us therefore come boldly to the throne of grace, that we may obtain mercy and find grace to help in time of need"* (Hebrews 4:16).

Once, when I was home in my office, my youngest daughter walked in to have me examine what was hurting her. As much as I wanted to send her out, I could not. I took care of her until all was well. Because she approached me in the confidence that I would help her, I was bound to do so by her confidence and trust. I dared not disappoint her trust in me for help. As a matter of fact, I used all that was available to me to make the pain go away. Well, God treats us the same. All of heaven's resources minister to our sincere requests for help. Go before your Father with what bothers you so that He can make it better. No matter the hurt, He will bring all of heaven's resources to restore you, if necessary.

Before we make a request of God, He knows about it. As man, He walked the earth, and He knows well the challenges we face daily. As God, He has the ability to change our present circumstances by reaching back into our past to fulfill His will in our lives for the future. God knows our future because He is already there, drawing us toward Him with each step we take. We have an appointment to appear before God with Christ Jesus. Live righteous and show up. Don't miss your appointment!

I Want to See Him for Myself

Certain Greeks who had come from Jerusalem to attend the Passover wanted to know how to find Jesus. *"Then they came to Phillip, who was from Bethsaida of Galilee, and asked him, saying, 'Sir, we wish to see Jesus'" (John 12:21).*

Although we may never have seen Jesus with our physical eyes, we have seen Him with our spiritual eyes by faith. We have seen Him walking the Judean hills. We have seen Him sitting upon the mountain, delivering the greatest sermon ever taught to man. We have seen Him praying fervently in the Garden of Gethsemane. We have seen Him bloodstained and covered with our sin in Pilate's court. We have seen Him hanging upon Calvary's cross. We have seen Him leaving the confines of an empty tomb and later ascending into glory.

Have you seen Him lately? Well, see Him answering your prayers, and He will. See Him healing your body, and He will. See Him bringing that job you requested of Him, and He will. See Him doing the miraculous, and get comfortable with it being normal in your life. Look beyond these pages into your heart for a fresh glimpse of our Lord. See Him for yourself!

At one time in my life, I said all the right things concerning prosperity, but I did not really see the Lord prospering me. When I began to study Scripture and recite it from memory, it got down into my heart. Then my faith for prosperity activated, and I saw God prospering me and my house. Meditating on the Word of God gave me a fresh glimpse of God's plan for prospering me. See Him for yourself doing great things for you, and He will! His ways and standards are much higher than ours.

Setting unusual standards has brought high recognition to the name of Jesus. Crowds flocked both to see and to hear His credible teachings, which challenged them to live life on a higher level. Scores of people followed Him. At the feast in Jerusalem, some Greeks wanted to get closer to Him because they had heard of His mighty works. This desire drove them into protocol, and they went directly to the disciples to gain access to Jesus. They got a chance to see and talk to Jesus. I am sure that the blessings they received by being in His presence were marvelous.

When men do unusual things, people flock to witness them. Michael Phelps won eight gold medals in the 2008 Beijing Olympics, attracting tremendous crowds to greet him wherever he goes. For the very first time in the history of the sport of swimming, someone had dominated multiple events at the level of excellence Phelps demonstrated.

When professional athletes come to town for competition, countless admirers and sports fans line the streets to catch a glimpse of them. People yearn to see the unusual. Things that we personally wish to accomplish and people we aspire to be have an intrinsic draw that attracts us. We are saying with our behavior that, because we have not achieved this feat yet, we at least want to see it. Or we think: *If I can see it, I can be it.* Unusual people and events will always headline the lives of men. The unusual serves as a measuring stick.

John the Baptist preaching in the wilderness was so unusual in mannerism and message that He emptied city after city as people journeyed to see him. John held the first conference ever, as people left home to hear the preaching of the gospel. Of all the places available, the last place most would come was the wilderness. Yet, the power and truth that laced every word John the Baptist spoke drew thousands to hear his teachings.

Now because this intrinsic attraction is true about these men, it is more so of Jesus. He has set the standard for the unusual. He had made the blind to see, the lame to walk, and the deaf to hear again. He had cleansed lepers and even raised the dead back to life. He tamed a Pharaoh to free Israel from the bondage of Egypt! Unusual events are a way of life for the Lord. He, to this day, has outdone everyone else. He alone has made the unusual become normal to those of us who believe in Him by faith.

What is extraordinary to the unbeliever is normal to the believer by faith in the supernatural power of God. To a true believer, what is unusual is someone who chooses to accept sickness, poverty, and defeat in his or her life. A believer has moved from the world's standard of unusual to kingdom normalcy. For a sick person to recover from illness is normal to a believer. For a person suffering poverty to achieve prosperity and success by faith and following biblical principles concerning finances is normal to a believer. For an underachiever to become a valiant, overachieving conqueror is normal to a believer.

Reasons for Seeking Him

Everything about Jesus was great. He was great in His preexistence, for He lived by His spirit before He was born of woman. He was great in His prophecy, for all the prophets pointed to His arrival into the world. He was great in His birth, for it was immaculate and void of the seed of man, like no other birth. He was great in His life, for He went about doing mighty works. He was great in His death, for He gave His life for those who were dead in sin. He was great in His resurrection, for He came to life from the dead, as no other could ever do. Jesus was, is, and forever will be the greatest person the world will ever know! He is the greatest light that has ever shone and the mightiest power the world has ever experienced. We should want to seek Him simply because of His greatness!

Seek Him because of His service and sacrifice. The blind man who receives sight through his surgeon's trained hands and skilled supervision wants to see the doctor and pay high regard for his expert care. A prisoner set free by a sitting governor would want to meet his liberator and thank him for that freedom. Jesus healed our blindness and gave us our spiritual eyesight, setting us free from sin and shame. For these reasons alone, we should want to seek Him.

The Bible records Jesus saying, *"But for this purpose I came to this hour" (John 12:27).* I want to make you aware that His every thought was of you and me. When we read that Jesus' sweat was as blood, we should remember that He was thinking about us. When He endured scourging all night long by Pilate's soldiers, He was thinking of us! When the crown of thorns punctured His brow, His thoughts were of us. He knew the suffering and pain ahead of Him and still accepted them on our behalf. As He cried, *"It is finished" (John 19:30)* on the lonely cross at Calvary, He was thinking of us. *"Most assuredly, I say to you, unless a grain of wheat falls into the ground and dies, it remains alone; but if it dies, it produces much grain" (John 12:24).* In predicting His own death, Jesus explained to us the divine purpose of His existence on earth. In order for us to become one with the Father, Jesus became the sacrificial offering and atoning blood for our sins. Why wouldn't you seek Him?

> I've heard it said that a man would climb a mountain
> Just to be with the one he loves.
> How many times has he broken that promise?
> It has never been done.
> Well, I never climbed the highest mountain,
> But I walked the hill of Calvary.

And just to be with you, I'll do anything,
There's no price I would not pay, no.
Just to be with you, I will give everything.
I would give my life away.

Third Day[8]

Seek Him by entering into the sessions of heaven. On earth, we are in a fight to keep righteousness as a foundation. Jesus is forever making intercessions on our behalf. We are battered and bruised on every side. To know that Jesus is constantly praying for me is a comfort to me. *"It is Christ who died, and furthermore is also risen, who is even at the right hand of God, who also makes intercession for us" (Romans 8:34).*

The Bible tells us that only one mediator stands between God and man, and I am glad that He is Lord of all. We no longer have to approach God through a priest, a church program, or a pious human agent. We have direct access through the precious life blood of our Lord and Savior Jesus Christ. *"I am the way, the truth and the life. No one comes to the Father except through Me" (John 14:6).* Oh, how I thank God for Jesus!

We have so many reasons why we should want to seek Jesus. I befriended a young man who later was incarcerated for a cruel crime. Prior to the criminal act, we spent time together as close friends. I was torn between hanging out with my dear friend and seeking a personal relationship with Jesus. I'm grateful that the Lord kept me from the unforeseen entanglement of his unfortunate downfall. He was an extremely smart, witty, athletic, and very personable individual who could have become anything he wanted to be. His decision not to seek after God has caused a lot of pain in his life and to those who cared for him. I thank God for drawing me in the direction He has. God is always gracious and merciful to us. Thank Him for His greatness. Thank Him right now for the things He has done, is doing, and will do for you. Thank Him for being your ever present mediator.

Voice of Authority

George Whitefield, a British evangelist, could speak certain words with his voice that would melt his audience to tears, and he preached about eighteen thousand sermons over the course of his life. John Wesley, the great theologian, evangelist, and hymn writer who founded Methodism, often spoke without the aid of a microphone to audiences of thirty thousand people at the age of seventy. Billy Graham's voice has been instrumental to counsel presidents and leaders around the world as well as to win millions to Christ. God continues to call to the premiere men and women in our day with distinct personalities and unique abilities to be voices of authority for Him. Bishop T.D. Jakes' persuasive and energetic voice dynamically influences listeners to connect their situations to the authority in God's word for restoration. Joel Osteen soothingly encourages many to turn to the grace of God. Dr. Frederick K. C. Price's confident and detailed biblical teachings have matured the understanding of millions around the world. Bishop Eddie L. Long's direct and sincere teaching method leaves his audience with the bottom-line choice of holiness. Marilyn Hickey's message of victorious living has impacted many the world over. Joyce Meyer's message of complete redemption in Jesus draws multitudes into the family of God. Dr. Myles Monroe's thought-provoking and intelligent presentations concerning God's kingdom business are having a mass impact on the world. The miraculous healing that many experience while basking in the direct presence of God under Benny Hinn's teaching is a wonder of God. The voice is a powerful vehicle that carries a message demanding change.

But something is more important than the voice. Something is even more important than charisma and stage presence. As gifted and talented as the speakers that I've mentioned are in their own right, what makes the difference is the message: what they say with their voice and the authority from which they draw. God spoke His approval over Jesus in the witness of others.

> *While they were still speaking, behold, a bright cloud overshadowed them; and suddenly a voice came out of the cloud, saying, 'This is My beloved Son, in whom I am well pleased. Hear Him!*
> *Matthew 17:5*

The Pharisees sent officers to arrest Jesus. As they came into the Garden of Gethsemane searching for Him, Jesus said, *"I am He" (John 18:6),* and the authority in His voice knocked them all down. The message was:

> *Therefore My Father loves me, because I lay down My life that I may take it again. No one takes it from Me, but I lay it down, and I have power to take it again. This command I have received from My Father.*
> *John 10: 17-18*

In other words, our Lord is saying, "I know that you brought a full regiment ready for battle to take Me. The truth is that you are weak, and you cannot take Me captive until I let you. Nonetheless, at My discretion, even after you have Me bound, I can set Myself free, and you cannot do anything about it! But I will let you have Me in order to fulfill My destiny in the Scriptures."

"Jesus is the same yesterday, today and forever" (Hebrews 13:8). The same truth He proclaimed over two thousand years ago stands true and appropriate today. Unless

you acknowledge your wrongdoings, repent, and turn from them, you will spend eternal separation from God.

In one of his sermons, my father told a powerful story about escaping separation from God. One night, a group of seminary students heard a fire engine go by. They followed the engine for blocks to a sanitarium engulfed in flames. Those students went in with the firefighters to help bring out the patients on the lower floors, and then they stood in front of the building. They heard screams coming from the rear of the burning building and rushed around to help. Upon arrival, they found four men trapped on the third floor, standing at the window, pleading for someone to save them from the flames. All ladders were in use, so four firefighters set up a net and called to the men, saying, "Leap down one at a time, and we will catch you."

The first three men leaped down to safety in the net. The fourth man drew back in fear, saying, "I am afraid to risk jumping into the net. Is there another way?" The firefighter and the students cried out, "The net is safe! Leap out, and we will save you." However, the man would not risk the jump. He turned back into the building, and the firefighters later found his charred body. The man failed to act on the instructions coming through the fireman's voice of authority to jump to his safety.

Men who fail to hear and follow the voice of God are in danger of eternal separation from Him. Only one way of escaping separation exists. You must repent of your sins and put your whole trust in God. This way is the only safe way. You cannot save yourself. Accepting and confessing what Jesus did for us is the only way. His net is safe. All you have to do is leap to Him in faith by following the instructions from His voice of authority, and He will safely catch and keep you in His everlasting care. Take the leap of faith now!

Chapter 4

Get to Higher Ground
Make the Change

I beseech you therefore, brethren, by the mercies of God, that you present your bodies a living sacrifice, holy, acceptable to God, which is your reasonable service. And do not be conformed to this world, but be transformed by the [renewing of your mind], that you may prove what is that good and acceptable and perfect will of God.

Romans 12:1-2

One of our nation's foremost authorities and living examples on the principle mentioned in Scripture of renewing the mind is pastor and teacher, Casey Treat. In 1998, my wife introduced me to his teaching on this principle, as she had been a long-standing member of Christian Faith Center in Seattle, Washington. I highly recommend getting your hands on any of his teachings and ministry resources, especially those on renewing the mind. His teaching has transformed my life to a new level. Subsequently, Wendy Treat's teaching on marriage and fatherhood from Proverbs 3:13-24 foundationally shaped my life as a husband and father of three.

Most people understand in theory the concept of renewing the mind. It is a commonly taught concept in both Christian and secular circles. However, implementing consistent daily activities to manifest the principle is where most people go wrong. If the process proved easy, the world would be in a far superior condition than it is at present. I submit to you that today's society has allowed itself to accept mediocre, status quo, good-enough-for-now standards. The effort that is required to cultivate character solid enough to persevere after God is just asking too much from a see it, get it, got it society.

I recall reading about the historical contribution that Chuck Yeager made to the world of aviation by being the first person to break the sound barrier officially. What a contribution! We now enjoy air commerce transportation, which tremendously decreases our time of travel. However, someone had to explore and experience the change from the norm. Yeager reported severe instability during the transition from normal speeds to breaking into supersonic speeds. Yeager chose to press through fear and doubt by enduring the violent shaking and horrible noises as the aircraft responded to the atmospheric pressure change in flight transition. Because he did, we enjoy modern, jet-powered aircrafts which spend a considerable amount of time in this new transonic state of travel.

Our lives are similar to Yeager's sound barrier-breaking flight experience. We encounter bumps, loud noises, and rigorous challenges that cause us to want to throw in the towel. Do not go there. If you are in a transition, giving up is neither an option nor the answer! Keep on putting one foot in front of the other until you walk through your challenge. Believe me, your path to destiny through this life is not all rocky roads. If you continue, it will smooth out. In order to change your view, you have to change both your mental state of mind and your physical location. Fight or flight: if you fight, then fight to win. If you take a fall, then get up and get back into the fight. DO NOT QUIT! Keep on fighting until you win. Whatever you do, do not just stand there and absorb the blows life throws at you. Fight back! Match the force of your opposition! Break barriers in your life that are preventing you from being all God has called you to be!

While attending Christian Faith Center, Pastor Casey taught exceptionally on renewing the mind. However, for me to take hold of that principle and make it work in my life took time. Isaiah 28:10 declares, *"For precept must be upon precept, precept upon precept, line upon line, line upon line, here a little, there a little."* I admit that renewing your mind is not an easy process, but if you stick to it, you will love the results. The transition takes place slowly, day-by-day, but it is attainable.

Change, however small or unnoticeable initially, is hard but inevitable. New is better than old! I had always found encouraging those around me to be a natural ability. My father set that example for me early in my life. As I prospered in my career, I had many opportunities to encourage and to prompt numerous people to advance well beyond my own position. Speaking words of encouragement into their lives, I've been blessed to witness their successes and sense their gratefulness. In the midst of my ability to encourage others, I knew that fear and doubt about my own abilities existed in me. To exercise faith for others was easy, because the risk of failure wasn't my burden to bear. I could believe for another to succeed; after all, if he didn't, his failure wasn't a reflection of my deficiencies. But God's Word is faithful when you are faithful to it. As I spent time reading about His promise for my life, faith eventually rose up inside of me and caused me to take God at His word.

> *For the word of God is alive and powerful. It is sharper than the sharpest two-edged sword, cutting*

between soul and spirit, between joint and marrow. It exposes our innermost thoughts and desires.
Hebrews 4:12 (NLT)

Now that I have broken the barrier of fear and doubt, my life has changed for the better. Challenges are still not easy, but I no longer deal with paralyzing fear and doubt. Just keep on walking out your faith, because as you walk it out, God works it out. I never want to miss another opportunity to synchronize my thoughts to God's. I want to accomplish all He has called me to be. You will never know what *all* is until you pursue it. Now that you know, make it happen!

You know the old Buddhist proverb: "When the student is ready, the teacher will appear."[9] Well, the Teacher, Jesus, has been there all along. The student needs to pursue Him with consistency, showing a high dedication to learning from the experiences and knowledge the Teacher has. If we do not change our way of thinking, we will never know what God has for us. He thinks and sees us on a much higher level than we usually see ourselves. Pursue change, and conquer mundane life. We find our destiny through this process of change.

My friend Grace owns a dry cleaner that I frequent for service. I took a pair of pants to be serviced, and while I was there, I asked her to adjust the waistline. She asked, "Why?" To which I replied, "My waist has gradually changed a few sizes too big." Grace quickly responded, "Then you need to make your waist a few sizes smaller." How true that statement is for most of us! All we have to do is reverse our circumstances to get back on track with our lives. More often than not, we allow life to go on until what should have been a small adjustment grows into a critical crisis.

In order to effect transformation from where you are at present to where you should be or want to be, you must think and move with purpose. Win the battle in your mind, and your body will manifest what your mind harbors. For example, picture five children sharing two bicycles; two of the five are riding. The others have never ridden a bicycle, and they joyfully run alongside or behind those with bicycles. Now in my picture, those who do not have a bicycle are happy to have the simple privilege of playing together. Once a child without a bicycle has the opportunity to ride, he or she discovers that the joy of riding equals or surpasses running. Suddenly, a new world of experience opens. Before, the kids without a bicycle were happy, unaware of a higher level of fun, but they occasionally wondered what the experience of riding is like. After getting on and falling off a few times, they can now ride, and they very much enjoy doing so. Probing questions always demand action. What would riding a bicycle be like? How can I? Has anyone done so before? Can I find a way to learn? My experience has been that you must be willing to pursue change in order to provide an answer to a question. The answer usually exists within the process of change. Just like the kids in this picture, we, too, should ask growing questions that challenge us to move into new activities which expose us to new levels of experiences in life.

Changing your thoughts to accept God's thoughts is a lifelong process. You never graduate, because only your capacity to receive and experience new ideas and concepts limits your growth potential. Isaiah 55:8 says, *"For My thoughts are not your thoughts, nor your ways My ways."* Get out of your mind and into God's. We have been living with inferior thoughts, which are beneath the high thoughts of God. We will have to train our thinking process to accept godly thoughts that are contrary to our way of thinking. Change requires effort. *"For as the heavens are higher than the earth, so are My ways higher than your ways, and My thoughts than your thoughts"* (Isaiah 55:9). Your effort must go beyond thoughts that do not line up with the principles of God. When you settle in a corner, your capacity to receive reaches a halt. Renew your mind to think like God about your life, and get out of the box inside which society has trapped you. As Robert Browning said, "A man's reach should exceed his grasp."[10] Do not settle for what's in front of you. Stretch out and explore other possibilities. You might like the adventure, as you may be able to choose from more opportunities, creating a whole new world for you!

My eight-year-old son and I were watching a TV show not long ago, and part way through the show, he said, "I don't like this show anymore." Immediately, the words came out of my mouth without thinking: "Change it; change the channel." All we have to do whenever we do not like what is happening in our situation is to change it! Assuming that your request for change agrees with God's plan, begin to implement the change. If you do not like your car, then change it! If you need a house with four bedrooms so that each of your three kids can have his own because you have outgrown the two-bedroom model, then change it! If you do not like how your friends talk to each other and act towards you, then change them! Are you getting this concept? When you do not like a situation, you have the right and authority to change it. Do not stay silent and suffer: CHANGE! Find that job you have wanted. Start that business you have been discussing and planning for the last five years. Move into a new neighborhood that will challenge you to grow. Make new friends. If your situation cannot be changed immediately, then begin to get vision for your change, and move toward it. If you desire a stronger marriage, which may require a process, then quickly begin to do things that cause your marriage to succeed. If you want to lose a few pounds, then that goal will not happen overnight. You have to get up and decide that you are going to change. Change the circumstances in your life through the words you choose to speak, the thoughts you allow to take residence inside your heart and mind, and the actions you take from the two. Collaborate the two without doubt and with consistency, and then watch heaven move on your behalf.

The weather in Seattle can slow things down to a grinding halt. When this interruption happens, those who dare to drive are careful to use vehicles that offer traction beyond two-wheel rear drive. The road conditions require extreme attention and a level of skill to maneuver a vehicle properly and safely. However, when the road conditions are back to normal operation, some drivers forget to change their driving habits. They continue to drive extremely slowly and cautiously, delaying normal traffic speed limits. I think that, from time to time, we do the same in our lives. We find a safe place and reject the needed change to get to higher ground. Be careful to pay attention to every season in your life and change as the seasons come. Don't get stuck in a rut.

Calvin Borel[11] quit school in the eighth grade to pursue his dream of becoming a jockey. Although his reading and writing skills were limited, he endeavored to change by becoming an equine expert. He succeeded by mastering his environment and reading horses. By age forty, Borel won the 2006 Breeder's Cup and the 2007 Kentucky Derby on a horse called Street Sense, which is the only colt to win both races in twenty-three years of competition. Subsequently, he received an invitation for dinner at the White House with President Bush and Queen Elizabeth. He made the transformation from a traditional to a nontraditional learning environment with great success! He focused his energy on training and his love of horses and competition, while making the necessary sacrifices to achieve his dreams. Change is inevitable, although it can start with you or come through circumstances.

Think Like God

The apostle Paul fought for God's thoughts, daily winning the battle of aligning his thoughts to God's. *"For I bear in my body the marks of the Lord Jesus" (Galatians 6:17).* Once the miracle of the mighty Savior's power touches your life, a life lived for Him becomes the evidence of this experience. No one is a better example of this truth than Paul.

From that brilliant day when he encountered Jesus on the Damascus highway, Paul's life exemplified service, with danger, with hardships, and with tremendous sacrifice. Someone has said that in every town where Paul went throughout his ministry, he had either a revival or a riot. At least something happened when he got there! He did not run from change or challenge. We see a similar character in David.

David did not like Goliath talking about God and Israel the way he did. David rejected the defeatist thinking of Saul's army, which did not want to do battle with the giant, and he changed the situation by slaying Goliath. When David walked into Saul's camp, he found the men hiding and refusing to engage the enemy for fear of Goliath. You see, Goliath had intimidated them with his size. Likewise, some things in life will intimidate us if we allow them to do so. So Saul's army sat still for days, brainwashed by Goliath that they could not defeat him until they believed his lie.

If you listen to a song long enough, even if you do not like the song, it will influence your thinking. David had to choose the high thoughts of God in order to take on the giant. So he started singing songs with truth like that in Romans 8:37, *"We are more than conquerors."* David remembered that God empowered him to kill a lion and a bear valiantly with his own hands while protecting his flock. He rehearsed his confidence in God like that in Isaiah 54:17, *"No weapon formed against you shall prosper."* Even though Goliath had a full set of body armor, sword, and shield, all that David had was an all-too-familiar sling.

David was convinced that professing the Word of God over his circumstances elevated his thinking to the level of God concerning Goliath. His changed thinking moved him to action. His action resulted in defeating the once incomparable and undefeated enemy. His valiant defeat of the enemy exposed his destiny. From this time on, David would have to perfect aligning his thinking to the thinking of God throughout the rest of his leadership days. The book of Psalms records this change as true.

After Paul repented of persecuting the church in Jerusalem, Paul pressed on with a champion's mindset to preach the gospel to the people followed by miracles, signs, and wonders talked about to this day. His perseverance changed the minds and hearts of the people in the face of persecution. The powerful and sustaining Word of God brings transformation everywhere it is preached. In order to sustain a ministry of this magnitude, Paul had to adjust his thinking to God's daily.

Outer Evidence

When Paul came to write his letters to the Galatians, the wounds of his conflict and the evidences of his sacrifice, which he acquired after earnestly committing himself to Christ, were upon his body. As he thought of his scars, he declared them proof of his love of and service for Jesus. At the end of this letter, he wrote in his own penmanship, *"For I bear in my body the marks of the Lord Jesus" (Galatians 6:17).*

The apostle was thinking of the cruel customs of that day, which allowed masters to brand their slaves. As we brand cattle today, so were men branded in days past. The burned initials of the master showing on the flesh of a man who was a slave kept everybody else away from him. That mark was the sign of his freedom from all other masters and his servitude to one. Another reference in the Bible about the mark of a slave occurs in the Old Testament. On New Year's morning of the seventh year of slavery, a man was made free under law. If, however, he so loved his master that he wanted to remain in his service, he would give himself into a new form of service. The master then would pierce his ear, signifying that this man was a slave who had gladly surrendered to service (see Deuteronomy 15:12-17). This practice is a very powerful analogy that Paul chooses to clarify his commitment to the gospel of Jesus.

With this custom of branding in mind, Paul contemplated the scars of battle on his hands, the marks of many lashes from whips on his back, and the wrinkles on his face. Then he said, in effect, "These scars indicate that I am the 'slave' (servant) of Christ, that I am free from every other master, and that my love and loyalty and my service all belong completely and without reservation to Christ, who is the Savior of the world." What deep and impenetrable devotion!

Now let's go deeper. I am convinced that every Christian should possess proof that he belongs to Christ. Surely, the world should see distinguishable differences between people who are in trivial pursuit and people who are living life under the influence of the cross! I am convinced that every Christian should carry credentials which verify a life committed to Jesus, something that signifies belonging to Jesus. This evidence is beyond a certificate, a creed, a church building where membership training occurred, or baptism through which we passed to give public notice of our faith in Jesus. I am talking about a deep change in which a man is constantly subduing his yearnings and making the spiritual supreme in everything he does.

Colossians 3:1 states: "*Set your mind on the things above, not on things on the earth.*" Put God, His will, and the service of His church ahead of everything else. The choice is ours. That to which we give our supreme affection works a change in our character. If I knew what you love most, whom or that to which you turn when all the barriers are down, or that which attracts your deepest loyalties and your finest enthusiasms, I would know the story of your life and the direction of your future. We are all slowly but inevitably becoming like the objects of our affection. That which we love most and to which we devote our supreme affection works a change at least in our personalities. Our experiences with good or evil leaves their marks upon us. The environment in which we allow ourselves to live does have a profound impact on our thinking. We often become products of our environment. Choose well; choose life. We become like that which we most love. So be like Paul and David; choose a life marked by evidence of living for Jesus.

Paul frequently spoke of his level of commitment to the Lord as being a "prisoner." In Ephesians 3:1, we find Paul describing himself as *"the prisoner of Christ Jesus."* Webster defines a prisoner as someone kept in custody, captivity, or a condition of forcible restraint in addition to depriving someone of freedom of action or expression.[12] Now we know that the letter of this definition does not pertain to Paul's status with the Lord.

The faces of freedom are many, based on each individual. John 8:36 says, *"If the Son makes you free [soul], you shall be free indeed."* This freedom identifies with joining the family of God, becoming joint heir with Jesus. Why would the Lord take Paul a prisoner after having set him free? After all, this freedom is the justification of His sacrifice on the cross: to free us from our sin and offer a higher life to our sin natures. I personally believe that, through faith in the gospel, a person could be incarcerated or jailed and still be set free within his cell space.

My soul has escaped the snare of the fowler.
I rise up on eagle wings to soar the great unknown.
The cares of this weary life are now far behind me.
I'm up above the shadows; I know where I belong.

<u>Chorus</u>
Living now,
Learning how,
To enjoy my life.
Being free from strife,
I'm totally out of bondage,
Since my soul has escape.

Nancy Harmon[13]

Romans 8:2 distinguishes two laws, *"For the law of the Spirit of life in Christ Jesus has made me free from the law of sin and death."* Freedom in this Scripture relates to walking life in the Spirit free from worldly condemnation. The law of the Spirit of Christ Jesus is GRACE! We received our salvation and freedom by the grace of God. We could never do anything that would serve as recompense for our flagrant disregard of God's standards and our sin before God. The law of sin and death is ETERNAL separation from God. Through grace, we no longer face separation from God, as our sins will be forgiven upon accepting the works of the cross.

You have to know that you are free to pursue righteousness continually. Galatians 5:1 states, *"Stand fast therefore in the liberty by which Christ has made us free, and do not be enlarged again with a yoke of bondage."* This level of freedom correlates to living a life free from the bondage of religious rituals, laws, and behaviors. We have been set free from religious laws established by man to govern and manipulate godliness. We should run from any governance that would snare us into that from which we were saved, and we would do well to perfect one principle of the Bible in our lifetime, specifically, *"This is My commandment, that you love one another as I have loved you" (John 15:12).*

Now the imprisonment analogy Paul uses to describe his relationship with the Lord is not as one would think. Paul is saying that he has bought into the truth of the gospel of Jesus because of personal, eyewitness exposure. In other words, Jesus is so very real to him in person that he has committed the rest of his life to His service. The only way he is able to explain the intensity of his submission to the Lord is by painting the picture of complete and total surrender equal to that of a prisoner. The height of his commitment surpasses the normal commitment made by the average person and the best of Christians. Paul has determined that serving the purposeful will of Jesus is all he desires out of life, no matter what it takes.

Another term Paul uses to describe his commitment is "bondservant." Webster defines a bondservant as one who is obligated to work without wages, or a slave.[14] We know that this condition was common in the Old Testament and still today in some countries. Some are servants as recompense for their bad behavior. Some are forced, and others serve in this capacity by choice. Paul made the commitment by choice after his one personal encounter with the Lord. He was convinced so many times throughout his life that the influence of his argument to live holy has stood, unsuccessfully rebutted, to this day. By taking on a slave or servant posture, Paul tremendously served God, ultimately writing two-thirds of the New Testament.

Paul's analogy of being a slave to Jesus illustrated what Christ did when He became a slave, our slave in love, giving Himself voluntarily to redeem us from the curse by way of the cross!

Inner Evidence

The true marks of a Christian are, after all, not external; they are internal! They are not outward; they are inward. Paul insists, *"For I bear in my body the marks of the Lord Jesus" (Galatians 6:17),* and *"Now if any one does not have the Spirit of Christ, he is not His" (Romans 8:9).* In other words, his profession, possession, and credentials all are without value unless he has the Spirit of Christ. Do you believe Jesus when He said, *"And if I be lifted up from the earth, will draw all peoples to myself" (John 12:32)?* Everyone who is a born-again believer should hear a challenge in this statement. I believe that we often miss the point. I believe that the Lord is saying, "I dare you to lift Me up. I dare you to let people see you lift Me up for who I AM. Take off all the limiting layers you have put on Me until I stand fully revealed for what I AM and who I AM in your life, and the world will come to Me." How are we to know when a man has been redeemed? Romans 8:13 says, *"For if you live according to the flesh you will die; but if by the Spirit you put to death the deeds of the body, you will live."* The daily choices you make will tell everyone about your life. I generally observe the behavioral choices of a person over time to know the status of his eternal commitment. The world does not look alone at the creed he recites, the words he uses, or the service he gives. Only after subduing his natural arrogance and walking before God in humility will he bear the marks of Christ. When he has a heart quick to repent and to seek the expressed will of God, influencing change through a circle of love big enough to include others before him, then, after developing these traits, his life begins to reflect the Spirit of Christ.

Committed

"*For whoever does the will of my Father in heaven is my brother and sister and mother*" *(Matthew 12:50).* Jesus made obedience to God the cornerstone of Christian living. We talk much these days about Christ as the Head of the church, Leader of radical change, Redeemer of man, Savior of the world, and Friend, but honestly, I do not think we talk enough about Him as Lord and Master. He is the Lord and Master of our lives. Salvation should yield fruits of obedience to the Word of God which lead to a life of righteousness with the ability to influence others. Do you read and study the Word of God daily?

> *For though by this time you ought to be teachers, you need someone to teach you again the first principles of the oracles of God; and you have come to need milk and not solid food. For everyone who partakes only of milk is unskilled in the word of righteousness, for he is a babe. But solid food belongs to those who are of full age, that is, those who by reason of use have their senses exercised to discern both good and evil.*
>
> *Hebrews 5:12-14*

Here we find a clear mandate to develop other key areas of our character while pursuing God and reading the Word. Our life should exemplify a demonstrative quality understanding of the Word of God. Others should want to mirror our discipline and determination to live a life of holiness with compassion for others, and adoration for Jesus as we share the gospel. We should attract others to the gospel through our lifestyle. Once we are skilled in the Word and living a life of righteousness, we then become friends.

No longer do I call you servants, for a servant does not know what his master is doing; but I have called you friends, for all things that I heard from My Father I have made known to you.

John 15:15

Are you committed to the kingdom of God? Righteousness comes through commitment. Commitment opens the door to intimacy. Jesus is saying, "I have told you intimate details from private conversations I have had with My Father because of your righteous commitment to Me and the Word of God." As you increase your commitment to Him, He releases valuable information to help you live for Him. Part of being committed is being set apart or consecrated to serve Jesus.

Consecration is a word that sounds spiritual to most but undesirable in action because of the sacrifice required. We come to the Lord kneeling, wiping tears from our eyes, and saying, "Here, Lord, I give myself to you, mind, soul, and body. My entire life I give to you. My time and my all are Yours to be used by You forever. Amen." Then we go to sleep or watch TV. Alternatively, we hit the refrigerator with no follow-through on that wonderful petition of prayer.

We acknowledge freely that God can help our lives, and we do give Him access to many of the rooms in our souls. However, we deny Him access to main corridors which give access to all other areas of our lives. Jesus must be the Master of all, or He will not be Master at all.

In the business of yielding ourselves in consecration to God, we do not yield to a cause or a creed; we simply give ourselves to God completely! Then He gives us our life assignments. In God, no place is small, and no task is unimportant. A prime credential of a Christian is obedience to God wherever He places you. Does your obedience to God attract others? Do your time, talent, resources, and ambitions belong to Him? Do you use them for His glory? How much room do you leave for self-pity, self-indulgence, and whining when your load gets heavy? Neglect partnership with such bad behavior. By doing so, you actively align your thoughts to the standard of God.

Do you genuinely love others? *"By this all will know that you are my disciples, if you have love for one another" (John 13:35).* We cannot be disciples and choose who we love in service to the Lord. We must see the whole world through the eyes of Jesus. His sacrifice and unconditional love for all peoples are the standards for those who love Him. The entire gospel hinges on the act of love. *"But if you love those who love you, what credit is that to you? For even sinners love those who love them" (Luke 6:32).* We cannot go around harboring malice toward anybody. It burdens and paralyzes our soul. Do you know what anger is? Anger is self-inflicted punishment that pursues someone for wronging you. That definition is the total sum of getting mad! Anger is just punishment you inflict on yourself for the stupidity of another. Let your anger drop to the ground, and forgive. Move through your mind-renewal process. Master it!

God paid a ransom to save us from the road to darkness and place us on the road to eternal life. The ransom was not gold or silver but the precious life blood of Jesus Christ. Because Christ Jesus cleansed our souls from selfishness and hatred, we should love each other warmly, with all of our hearts. Choose to love and live. If love is at the beginning of our lives, it will be at the end of our lives. We will do well to live in love toward each other.

What will you sacrifice? Jesus Himself defined the necessary sacrifice in Mark 8:34, *"Whoever desires to come after Me, let him deny himself, and take up his cross, and follow Me."* Not until we can do the will of the Father, love the Lord Jesus, follow Him, and shoulder our cross daily, can we be called disciples of Christ. Jesus carried the sins of the whole world on His shoulders. He is not asking us to do what He did by carrying the entire load. Nonetheless, we should remember the responsibility Jesus left for us all to share. *"Go into all the world and preach the gospel to every creature" (Mark 16:15).* We can never shoulder our Christian responsibilities without aligning our thoughts to His. To answer the question concerning sacrifice, we must first permit the Holy Spirit to examine us to know what is in the sincerest part of our hearts.

Obedience, love, and sacrifice are the three basic tests we will all face during the process of changing into the image of Christ. Of the three tests, love is the foundation. I accept you in brotherhood, and purpose to help you. In fact, I am so eager to help you that I will share what I have or temporarily deny myself to ensure you get what you need. Sacrifice is the crowning credential, because it is proof of obedience and love. These three essentials describe the unmistakable stamp upon Christians anywhere in the world. They enable us to say, "I belong to Jesus. Here are the results of my test; I passed!" We find complete freedom in living for God. Get your mind free!

You know what Thomas said when the other disciples told him that the Lord had risen. *"Unless I see in His hands the print of the nails, and put my finger into the print of the nails, and put my hand into His side, I will not believe" (John 20:25).* He wanted to relive the crucifixion of Jesus himself before he believed. Thomas had to put his fingers in the wounds, and Jesus did not object. Thomas should have agreed with the fresh move of God and believed as the others did. Because he did not, Jesus submitted Himself to the test so that Thomas could believe.

The scars that Paul had worn were no longer scars; they became tributes proving that he endured the process of aligning his life to the will of God. He was proud of them. "See that place? That mark is where they beat me at Philippi.

The wound over here, remember? I got that one in Damascus getting over the wall in a basket." His scars became a tribute. He became as proud of them as most men are of their accomplishments. What marks of the Lord Jesus do you wear? Are you too proud to display them? Are you battle worthy? Are you part of His army? Have you pledged your allegiance to His kingdom cause? You see, if you never fight, you run no risk of injury or battle wounds. If you stand for nothing, you will fall for anything. Make a commitment! Dedicate your life to His service, and experience unspeakable joy as He changes you in order to change the world with the gifts, talents, resources, and remaining time that you have.

Fight for Holiness

In times past, Christians have suffered countless persecutions. Today offers no change. Our Lord warned us of such attacks concerning the gospel. Clearly, holiness is God's minimum standard to set us, those He has saved, apart from the world. We have been separated from sinful behavior and "called out." In the middle of life with its many trials, we must continue living in holiness, for God has reserved the priceless gift of eternal life with Him for those who do so. For those of us who read His words and obey His instruction, this life will prove successful.

> *This Book of the Law shall not depart from your mouth, but you shall meditate in it day and night, that you may observe to do according to all that is written in it. For then you will make your way prosperous, and then you will have good success.*
> *Joshua 1:8*

However, you will have to fight daily to preserve your life with holiness. Choosing to meditate on the Word of

God means you are not continually thinking on things in the world. This practice is nothing new for most, but we press for it daily. Just remember that the enemy wants you to slip and return to emptiness, and do not falter. Fight back, knowing that God loves you with an enduring passion which all the wiles of the evil one cannot quench. God knows of your challenges in this life. Allow the Holy Spirit to enable you to live in love with everybody and to keep you in a state of holiness. You can succeed! Keep in mind that God has no favorites when He judges. The Lord will judge everything we do with perfect justice, and *"He who has begun a good work in you will complete it until the day of Jesus Christ" (Philippians 1:6).* His faithfulness to us is without end.

> Great is thy faithfulness, O God my Father,
> There is no shadow of turning with Thee.
> Thou changest not, Thy compassions, they fail not;
> As Thou has been, Thou shall forever be.
> "Great is Thy faithfulness!"
> Morning by morning, new mercies I see;
> All I have needed, Thy hand hath provided,
> "Great is Thy faithfulness," Lord, unto me!
> William M. Runyan[15]

Chapter 5

Ambassadors for Christ
Why Am I Here?

⚜

Our lifelong commitment, as ambassadors for Christ, is to influence the world with the Good News of the gospel unto salvation. *"Now then, we are ambassadors for Christ, as though God were pleading through us: we implore you on Christ's behalf, be reconciled to God" (2 Corinthians 5:20).*

The president of the United States cannot be everywhere simultaneously. Therefore, he appoints ambassadors to represent abroad his authority and the best interests of our country. Once the president appoints his ambassador to duty, only the president can remove that ambassador: he has a presidential appointment. As such, the ambassador is accountable for everything he says and does while carrying out his duties.

Although I have always had the capability to influence people, I did not know how to use my abilities to carry out the duty of winning souls. Now I clearly understand that, as ambassadors for Christ, we are obligated to act within His authority to win souls. We have the exact responsibility to influence the world with the Good News of the gospel as

Jesus did. A part of the greater works Jesus talked about is that we, as a corporate body, reach the multitudes He did not reach prior to His ascension. So I say to you, "Madam Ambassador or Mister Ambassador, learn to use your influence to win souls for Jesus." This is why it is so important for you to consistently attend and support a bible teaching church. You must be taught how to fulfill your ambassadorial duties.

Because the winning of souls is so important to God, every request we make should support and center around this campaign. Matthew 7:7 says, *"Ask, and it will be given to you; seek, and you will find; knock, and it will be open to you."* I believe that this Scripture speaks of revelation knowledge concerning God's eternal plan to win souls.

If you and a friend have collaborated to accomplish a task of which you both have common knowledge but find your resources inadequate to complete the task, then you need to recruit additional partnership. Before your partnership takes on a third party, the new member needs to be updated on the vision of the project after being personally assessed to determine whether he or she is the right fit for the partnership. When approved, he or she will have earned the right to the next level of critical information in the partnership.

God has every resource needed to accomplish His soul-winning campaign except volunteers. He needs every one of us to share the Good News with someone to win him or her over to Christ. Our prayers go through screening by the Holy Spirit prior to accessing the next level of critical information required to win souls in masses. Anyone with sincerity for winning souls is an ambassador for God. Prepare yourself so that God can trust you at the next level, and He will provide you many opportunities to share the gospel of Christ. He values each soul so highly that, if you are willing, available, and prepared, He will bring people to you. Pray with a deep, burning desire to see others saved, and God will use you in His salvation campaign.

We all share a common charge, which is to expose the gospel to every breathing soul. Until we accomplish this charge, Jesus will not return. We often rehearse that we are waiting on Him. My understanding of our role indicates that He is waiting on us to spread the gospel to every nation, people, and language. Let's give ourselves over to this focused task. Win souls everywhere you go, under all circumstances, in every situation, at all cost, at all times!

To make a long story short, I recently resigned at the pinnacle of my career for lack of being used to my potential. Every day, the thought of going to work made me depressed. I thought that there had to be more to life than the temporary relief of having a job. My need for more created a void within me that could only be filled by a source higher than everything ever offered to me. My thoughts puzzled me, because most people would love to be second in charge of a large organization making well over a six-figure salary. The position and compensation could not soothe my ache to know God as I had never known Him.

After leaving my job, I began a ravenous feeding on the Word of God by reading ten to twenty chapters of the Bible a day, sometimes not stopping until the next morning. I fasted and prayed with a clear focus. The more I read with understanding, the deeper and more frequent revelation came. Things of God became much clearer and more obvious to my spiritual eyes. Unusual doors began to open, as they still do to this day. I am amazed! Identifying the cause of my void did not take long. When I discovered that a call was on my life to use my influence in working directly for God, everything offered to me paled in comparison.

I am sure I missed a few good opportunities; however, I had to know for myself my call, destiny, and purpose through opportunities from God. I recently established an organization to train, employ, and mentor the homeless and young adults while compiling this book simultaneously. Oh, what a relief I find in pursuing God, and in my lane! Great things are happening as I pursue His will for my life. I believe that these events are avenues leading me closer to what He has predestined. I will continue to use my influence to win the lost while fulfilling destiny.

My earnest plea to you is: **DO NOT** just accept your circumstances or settle where you are! Don't you dare settle for less than your promise from the mouth of God, especially if it is short of your destiny. Find your place, and get there! Life happens quickly. If you are not careful, life will overwhelm you with trivial things that move you into a place of mediocrity where you boast that you are not doing badly, while you are dying of decay inside for not living your purpose. Believe me; I spent an empty season there. Well, are you doing any good? Good is okay until you place it next to better. Better is all right until you place it next to outstanding. Outstanding has a place until excellent overshadows it. You get the picture. Keep on moving right into perfect!

Wait on Him

All born-again Christians should wait on the Almighty God until they identify their individual destinies. This waiting is often unnecessarily a long and tedious process for most, but it does not have to be. *"The spirit of God hath made me, and the breath of the Almighty hath given me life" (Job 33:4).* God has a specific, predestined assignment for each of us. You must pursue and find yours. When you do, it will take you through life like a whitewater rafting excursion. Just enjoy the ride, and paddle like mad. You are the only one that can do what God called you to do. Find your assignment and do it! Many are waiting on the other side of your obedience to God.

Your purpose in life is so specific and critical to the winning of souls that, when God created you, He had this specific job in mind. Ask God the Holy Spirit to give you revelation knowledge about your personal obligation within God's soul-winning campaign.

That the God of our Lord Jesus Christ, the Father of glory, may give to you the spirit of wisdom and revelation in the knowledge of Him, the eyes of your understanding being enlightened; that you may know what is the hope of His calling.

Ephesians 1:17

This discovery is not up to God. You must pursue God for what He has stored up for you.

His Desire

"But seek first the kingdom of God and His righteousness, and all these things shall be added to you" (Matthew 6:33). Cultivate a heart of desire for the things of God! God has promised to help you align your desires to His. *"I will give you a new heart and put a new spirit within you; I will take the heart of stone out of your flesh and give you a heart of flesh" (Ezekiel 36:26).* Here God describes a surgery of the supernatural variety. While God can give you a new physical heart, He won't do so in this case; He is talking about your desires. The "new heart" in this passage of Scripture is analogous of God revealing His burning desire to you. The "new Spirit" is symbolic of God giving you His energy, determination, courage, and strength to focus on the one thing that He wants you to do. Additionally, He wants to prepare you for success and to help you succeed at the same time. He

gives you His desires and accomplishes them through you. What a deal!

God expects us to use our intelligence, emotions, and faith to accomplish His desire for our lives.

But also for this very reason, giving all diligence, add to your faith virtue, to virtue knowledge, to knowledge self-control, to self-control perseverance, to perseverance godliness, to godliness brotherly kindness, to brotherly kindness love. For if these things are yours and abound, you will be neither barren nor unfruitful in the knowledge of our Lord Jesus Christ.
2 Peter 1:5-8

Recently, I was preparing a meal for my kids the way they liked it. After I started the recipe to prepare the meal they had requested, they went to another level of creativity. They started asking for all kinds of food with multiple fixings. I tried to be flexible and flow with them; so I changed a few times to appease them. The changes started out being fun. But a few minutes later: not so much. Suddenly, I got revelation knowledge on how we treat God, hindering our petition. With much excitement, we spontaneously ask God for something. As any Father would, God starts the process to bring our reasonable request to fruition. During the process, we change our minds. Well, I believe that God does what He revealed to me while I was feeding my kids. He either gives us what we should have, setting aside our impetuous requests, or delays His answer until we have a clear picture with a burning desire for it. Every time my kids changed their minds, they caused me to start the process of making their meal all over, delaying their receiving and eating time. Subsequently, they complained of hunger until the food was served. My wife would have simply prepared the right meal for them the first time and told them to enjoy their meal. When our desired request is in the right vein but with the wrong details, I believe that God steers us in a direction which leads us to the perfect sight picture alignment needed to grant His desire for us through our petition.

Soul Winning

Presidential candidates gain support and win elections based on their campaign agendas. Those that effectively promote and publicly defend the critical elements of their plans are sure to be elected, because they will have aligned their comprehensive plans to the needs of the masses. Well, we know that God rules the universe without election, appointment, or promise from anyone. He is God all by Himself because He is! *"I am the Lord, that is My name; and My glory I will not give to another, nor My praise to carved images" (Isaiah 42:8).* Hallelujah, God has launched an active and vibrant soul-winning campaign to restore man to spiritual wholeness!

The greatest campaign ever known and implemented is God's plan to regenerate the whole of man from the stained grips of sin and shame. He has promoted this comprehensive plan with the best marketing promotion to date. Nothing is more effective and compelling than the power of personal testimony. When God the Father, God the Son, and God the Holy Spirit agreed to offer one-third of the kingdom of God (Jesus, His only begotten Son) as a sacrificial offering, the world saw and continues to experience a supreme level of marketing.

God the Son (Jesus Christ) left heaven to walk among man with the guidance and help of God the Father and God the Holy Spirit to testify (give a firsthand, personal, eyewitness account) of the Father's love to reconcile sinners unto Himself. Jesus also testified of His forgiveness to save man from eternal condemnation and destruction from the evil one. Jesus took on the form of man in order that He might become the perfect sacrifice to allow regeneration and spiritual transformation of man. When Jesus hung on the cross, he cancelled the curse of sin in our lives. We have been redeemed by His life's blood, which was shed at Calvary.

The redeemed of the Lord are joint heirs with Christ to the throne of God. Further, we are commissioned to continue Jesus' ministry to the lost. *"Now all things are of God, who has reconciled us to Himself through Jesus Christ, and has given us the ministry of reconciliation" (2 Corinthians 5:18).*

The Perfect You

"How precious also are thy thoughts unto me, O God! How great is the sum of them" (Psalms 139:17). I want to help you understand that God did not wake up late as a college student, piece you together, throw you into this world, and say, "Here it is; it might work!" Quite to the extreme contrary, God counseled Himself with Jesus and the Holy Spirit prior to lifting a creative finger to design you. *"Let Us make man in Our image, according to Our likeness" (Genesis 1:26).* Now, we know that we are not His exact image because we have a body; and because only one God can exist. And He does. However, our ability to think and speak intellectually, our sensual discernment, and our spiritual communion with God all bear His likeness. We have a mind, body, and soul with the mandate and ability to act with dominion over the earth. Obviously, the body is necessary as clay vessel to house the spirit and to meet the requirements of this world as a human being.

Think about this truth: in order for God to have created you with perfection to fulfill your destiny, He had to consider everything He created before you, everything in existence during His detailed creation of your person, everything prearranged, and every anticipated future event predestined to take place beyond your creation. We know that God is infallible, but if He had miscalculated one infinitesimal detail, you would be a mistake, because you would not fit into the ebb and flow of His divine master creation of the world. Instead of adding to creation, you would impede, frustrate, and I dare say interrupt His flawless plan for the distribution of the gospel.

Think about it. Jesus participated in the creation of the world. While He scooped out the waterbeds for the sea, He simultaneously heaped wondrous mountains. The logistics alone before adding life is miraculous. He purposed to create man with a mind, soul, voice, and a balanced upright frame. Subsequently, these features are unique to all others in creation. Have you ever wondered why? This same Jesus healed the leper, gave sight to the blind, and brought life to the dead. He fed multitudes with a few fishes and loaves of bread. He stilled a raging storm and quieted the waves of the raging sea. Surely He has the ability to perfect our lives in Him if we participate with His process. Listen, if you just take what He has given you and put it to use in His service, He will reveal the details!

To the best of my knowledge, heaven has no reject baskets. Therefore, you must accept that you are His perfection to fulfill God's great purpose. Psalm 139:14 says, *"I will praise thee; for I am fearfully and wonderfully made: marvelous are thy works; and that my soul knoweth right well."* Take inventory, and you will quickly find that no other creation of God can match the dominion of man or enjoy a relationship with the Father as we do.

In the eyes of God, we are perfect. He does not see us as we see ourselves. He is waiting on us to act like He created us: in His image. He has always been willing to help us be what He created us to be, even to the point of restoration.

"And the vessel that he made of clay was marred in the hand of the potter; so he made it again into another vessel, as it seemed good to the potter to make" (Jeremiah 18:4).

Remember when Apollo 13 encountered a severe interruption to its space flight plan? It lost the power necessary to reenter earth's atmosphere and suffered external damage to the ship, which then had limited oxygen supply for the crew. Mission control on the ground quickly assessed the damage in relation to what the crew needed to ensure a return entry into the earth's atmosphere, inventoried the supplies onboard that were significantly useful to overturn the demise, and recreated a duplicate environment using those same supplies to produce an extreme makeover of the craft to bring the crew home.

God did the same thing through Jesus for us. After we lost dominion on earth through sin, suffered physical loss and spiritual damage to our relationship with Him, which left us no strength or power to fight the enemy, He restored us. He picked us up in His great big hands, saw that we were marred, and then: *"He made us again another vessel as it seemed good to Him."* He fully restored us with dominion, power, and His authority to reign over creation and rule earth. We got an extreme makeover with the perfection and affection of God the Creator!

His Thoughts

Our God is an awesome God!
He reigns from heaven above
With wisdom power and love.
Our God is an awesome God!

Rich Mullens[16]

A divine wisdom flows down from the Creator to benefit the overall harmony of man. When God guides us to think

His thoughts, which lead to right action and bring fruitful results, we must consider the source of those thoughts. *"In the beginning God created the heavens and the earth" (Genesis 1:1).*

God is invulnerable in His thinking. He consistently executes infallible activities. His ways and thoughts towards us are immutable. He is immune from the petty logic and intellect of man. His universal and kingdom principles are immovable and unimpeachable. God is the only one who can materialize His thoughts through the process of creative speech. He is sovereign and accountable to Himself.

> *Who has directed the Spirit of the Lord, or as His counselor has taught Him? With whom did He take counsel, and who instructed Him, and taught Him in the path of justice? Who taught Him knowledge, and showed Him the way of understanding?*
>
> *Isaiah 40:13-14*

At His own inspiration, God's thoughts will frequently interrupt and override our thought process. When we faithfully proclaim God's overriding thoughts verbally, He brings them to pass! Your speech allows the supernatural to invade the natural, creating a heavenly charged atmosphere for the Holy Spirit to work miracles. Your thought process and verbal speech are super highways by which the transportation of miraculous cargo from heaven travels into your NOW situation or present circumstance to fulfill God's will on earth as it is in heaven. Speak the Word always! God can take one person speaking and operating in faith and change the world.

> *For if by one man's offense death reigned through the one, much more those who receive abundance of*

grace and of the gift of righteousness will reign in life through the One, Jesus Christ.
Romans 5:17

Jesus proclaimed the Word of God to regenerate the whole of mankind in its entirety! He did not claim just one but all.

God does not operate with a single-task temperament. He is the ultimate multitasker. When He rescues you, He saves thousands. He reduces the intellect of academic circles and master chess players to child's play. When He heals you, your testimony and the witness of your healing inspire others to the possibility of miracles in their lives. When He blesses you, everyone around you ready for a blessing receives one. God's blessing is a family affair! God does not limit His blessings to one person ever. However, we consistently limit His open willingness to bless us with closed minds and small thoughts. He has too many family members to bless us one at a time. We would all die, just as the people of Israel would have in the desert upon exiting Egypt, waiting our turn to be blessed with such small thinking.

How about this thought? If God brought Israel out of Egypt one person at a time, one million plus, the exodus operation would still be in high gear today! Well, if you believe that God does things one at a time, then you had better get as close as you can to the front of the line, because the wait will be extremely long. If He did the same thing for the crossing of the Red Sea while Pharaoh was in hot pursuit, the pillar of fire would still be burning, and maybe number three hundred fifty thousand would just be taking the first step of thousands to cross the floor of the Red sea. Oh, my friends, you do not have to delay your wait on God beyond your measure of active faith. Faith is NOW! To see the gates of Egypt or the mouth of the Red sea open and only witness one person at a time take passage to freedom would do me no good.

God does not work in that way. He uses every situation effectively to change lives. We limit God through our small thoughts about His majestic abilities. Not only does the change affect the direct receiver, it also indirectly influences those in the vicinity who have an expressed interest. Those witnessing the miracle of Jesus raising Lazarus from the dead were persuaded into full belief as they saw Lazarus leave the opening of the grave. When Jesus turned water into wine at the wedding, the quality of the miracle converted hundreds of hearts and minds. Upon receiving sight, the blind man publicly declared that Jesus healed him, and he was not concerned about how. *"One thing I know, that, whereas I was blind, now I see" (John 9:25).* Do not analyze your miracle; just receive it!

Whatever your current situation, do not take a number and wait like a small-thinking person would have you do. Obey the Word of God, and receive your very own right-now-turn-around-in-the-middle-of-your-circumstances blessing. Even as you read this book, God is reversing your situation and turning it around for your good and the good of those near you. He never blesses you alone. His blessing is a family affair. Would you as a mother prepare dinner for only one of your three kids, or would you as a father only teach one of your two sons to drive a car? No: if you bless one, then you want all to share in the blessing. This principle, that blessing for many always comes through one, is in line with God's way of thinking and His divine process for salvation.

Accordingly, He takes great care to plan the details of our lives to maximize our creative potential in order to mature and bless others around us. Usually, when you have a thought from God, it is not solely for you. However, you will benefit through the unfolding and manifestation of the thought. God thinks of you and everyone else simultaneously within each individual thought that enters His insoluble mind. We can only think of one person or a combined group of people in a single thought. God thinks in delicate details about everyone, everywhere, concerning everything at the same time. He is the foundation to everything that was, is, and ever will be. He is infinite in all His ways. Nothing is too hard for God. He does what He does because no one else can! He is a self-sufficient God! No one else is like Him. Amen.

Your Destiny

When God ordains an activity or event, rest easy and know that He has given thought to every possible outcome. The fact that we act as stewards of one of His many campaigns to win souls indicates that He is in total control. God allows us to sit shotgun to witness His miracles. In and of ourselves, we could do very little to bring about any noticeable change along the lines of winning souls for the kingdom. The fact that resources provide for ministry needs goes without saying. God has no shortage of resources and no limit on what He will finance to promote His soul-winning campaign.

I believe that God views resources in three basic categories. Every born-again believer must exercise good stewardship over the resources from His treasury in order to accomplish His expressed will.

First and foremost, we must use the resources that He entrusts to us to inform the whole world about Jesus Christ and about all spiritual truths concerning the kingdom of God. Simply put, we must spread the gospel. *"For the Son of Man has come to seek and to save that which is lost" (Luke 19:10).* Until everyone has had an opportunity to hear and decide for themselves about the gospel of Jesus, we pursue every occasion to fulfill Scripture concerning reaching the world for Jesus!

Secondly, we must use heavenly resources from God's storehouse to stop and to destroy the works of the evil one. The devil loves sin, and he uses many vices to entrap and ensnare the people of God. God knows that evil exists in our world, and He has purposefully put measures in place to defeat it if we avail ourselves of His wisdom, His ways, and His instructions for our resources.

> *He who sins is of the devil, for the devil has sinned from the beginning. For this purpose the Son of God was manifested, that He might destroy the works of the devil.*
>
> *1 John 3:8*

Thirdly, God has prearranged resources from His heavenly distribution center to provide abundance for His people. Those who consistently honor Him with the first fruits of all that they manage while cultivating the lifestyle of a generous and cheerful giver are particularly prosperous. *"The thief does not come except to steal, and to kill, and to destroy. I have come that they may have life, and that they may have it more abundantly" (John 10:10).* We should be living full and happy lives absent poverty, depression, and lack.

God never intended for His children to be in want or to lack for anything. *"Beloved, I pray that you may prosper in all things and be in health, just as your soul prospers"* (3 John 2). Preaching the gospel, destroying the works of the enemy, and living in abundance sounds like "prosper in all things" to me! Notice the order of importance in the list. God is foremost, and then we meet the needs of others before ourselves. I believe that if we keep this perspective throughout our lives in this order, then every born-again Christian should experience the abundance of God the Father. In every area, our lives should reflect the life that Jesus modeled before us. Our Lord and Savior made a way for us!

Serve with a Loyal Heart

Keep in mind that putting your heart into all that you do will lead to promotion and increase. *"And whatever you do, do it heartily, as to the Lord and not to men, knowing that from the Lord you will receive the reward of the inheritance; for you serve the Lord Christ" (Colossians 3:23-24).* In 1995, I left Boston to accept a teaching position at the FAA Academy in Oklahoma City. The academy recognized my love for imparting knowledge with zeal. This faith in me was a tremendous blessing, because I did not have the full-rated credentials to teach at the time. After accepting the job, I earned the proper certification.

However, I had the grace and favor of God. The academy offered me the position of lead instructor with the assignment of managing the fast-paced training regimen required for all employees in the security division of the agency. I worked hard during long hours with a focused drive, and I had lots of fun along the way! Everyone around me tapped into my enthusiasm, which elevated their lives and the lives of those they influenced. Why? I served my supervisor as if I were working for Jesus Himself. The participants in each class I managed excelled and looked forward to coming back for additional training! No corners were cut, and no stone was left unturned. At the end of my day, I could not wait until the next morning to get started again! I simply love people. Serving others brings me unspeakable joy! My assignments set my daily agenda items that brought great accomplishments and generous compensation.

Unlike man, God knows our deepest inner motives. 1 Chronicles 28:9 says, *"Serve Him with a loyal heart and with a willing mind; for the Lord searches all hearts and understands all the intent of the thoughts."* While serving with loyalty and willingness, I met my wife on this assignment, and we have been happily married for over ten years with three wonderful kids! Give God your best at all times, and He will give you His best always.

> *Give and it will be given to you: good measure, pressed down, shaken together, and running over will be put into your bosom. For with the same measure that you use, it will be measured back to you.*
> Luke 6:38

In fact, if you make a habit of serving with your best effort, then you can expect God's best in return, running over even to overflowing. The words in the Bible are His words. That being the case, you can trust Him in all that He says. "God is not a man, that he should lie, nor a son of man, that He should repent. Has He said, and will He not do? Or has He spoken, and will He not make it good?" (Numbers 23:19).

Some job assignments are less visible than others. You may think that your job is boring and lacks exciting action compared to some. For example, military personnel during times of peace may experience a sense of boredom and long for excitement. However, the importance and vitality of their job assignments shows in conflict. Thank God for our men and women serving in the armed forces, and may they forever be vigilant and protected under the mighty hands of God.

Prioritize

My wife is like God; she can work in chaos to produce the miraculous. I tend to want things neat and organized prior to doing anything. For example, if I use a computer, chances are I will spend a considerable amount of time in preparation. I have to put every sheet of paper away in its right location and file the books in order before I sit at the computer. I have recently found this tendency to be a waste of my valuable time. I get sidetracked into cleaning everything. Now, a stack of everything out of the way will do just fine.

    I have learned to let the dishes and the laundry sit, because they will be there after I am through with other important things. I found myself washing dishes and laundry only to wash more dishes and laundry. The cycle is a perpetual necessity that should not take the place of important matters. As a server, I have had to train myself to focus on matters of importance. *"Martha, Martha, you are worried and troubled about many things. But one thing is needed, and Mary has chosen that good part, which will not be taken away from her" (Luke 10:42).* The Lord says to prioritize your activities based on importance and mass influence. If you do so, your destiny will become clear and obvious to you and others. Focus on the thing you love most to produce the largest influential impact for the kingdom!

    A man had to journey across a sun baked desert to reach his next destination. After a period of enduring the punishment of direct exposure from the sun and being robbed of hydration from the dry and dusty desert winds, he reached an abandoned town. In the center of town was a water pump with a small jar of water and a cardboard note leaning against it. The note simply read, "DO NOT DRINK – PRIME THE PUMP". I'll remind you of his unbearable and what must have seemed like unquenchable thirst from his journey. His dilemma was whether to drink the last gulp of water in sight selfishly or to follow the instructions on the note. By following the instructions of the note, he would meet his need, and he would provide for others who were sure to follow by priming the pump first, drinking his thirst away, and leaving the jar full with the note just like he found it.[17]

God Is Your Source

Recognize that God is the source of sustenance and that all that you have belongs to Him. *"But who am I, and who are my people, that we should be able to offer so willingly as this? For all things come from You, and of Your own we have given You" (1 Chronicles 29:14).* The revelation here is that God gave you what you give to others and to Him. God is the sole source of everything you have now, had in the past, or ever will have in the future. Never forget that He is unlimited in all things. He is the source of your supplies. *"Now may He who supplies seed to the sower, and bread for food, supply and multiply the seed you have sown and increase the fruits of your righteousness" (2 Corinthians 9:10).* If He did not allow you to possess what you have or give it to you, you would not have the sum total of all your possessions. Recognize this truth, and honor Him with your best always.

Remember to bless God with the first portion of all your increase. *"And you shall remember the Lord your God, for it is He who gives you power to get wealth, that He may establish His covenant which He swore to your fathers, as it is this day" (Deuteronomy 8:18).* God wants you to be blessed in order to be a blessing to others. You are a part of His eternal family. As the Father of all, He has already made provisions for us. We need only to pursue, to possess, and to tap into what belongs to us as our Heavenly Father provides it. Wise stewardship of God's resources will ensure that everyone who believes and trusts will receive by faith the provisional blessings that the Father has made available to each.

Chapter 6

Love with a Prayerful Heart
Pray with Clear Focus

∽●∾

I want to share something with you that I recently discovered. While I am certainly not the first one to discover this truth, for the first time I have been able to tie it into recent results that I have seen in my life. I have discovered that when you pray for others, you attract the favor of God to yourself. I do not suggest that you do so selfishly, because you would be operating outside of faith. When you pray for others with a focus to see them sincerely blessed, your needs materialize in the process. Two Scriptures come to mind.

"Therefore I exhort first of all that supplications, prayers, intercessions, and giving of thanks be made for all men" (1 Timothy 2:1). The Lord has purposed us to be knitted together through the works of the cross, Christian fellowship, and continual prayer. Prayer is a dynamic means of communication with God. Through our prayer lives, the Lord monitors and listens compassionately as we verbally express our sincere desires. When our desires become one with His, He consummates the union by intensifying our petition, preparing us to take guided action to advance His kingdom. Pray for others as part of your petition.

If you sow prayers, then others will pray for you. You may not know who is praying for you. Because this prayer is the will of God, He makes the assignment of your intercessor. If you sow prayers for others, others will be praying for you. Better yet, God appoints someone as the answer to your prayers. Wow! This concept is simple, but very effective. Jesus prayed without ceasing for the twelve with astonishing results.

God always responds to faith regardless of the amount. Hebrews 11:6 states, *"But without faith it is impossible to please Him, for he who comes to God must believe that He is, and that He is a rewarder of those who diligently seek Him."* God is serious about the business of our seeking relationship with Him. He created us to be very successful through the camaraderie of being in relationship with Him and others. When you really love someone, your prayers can help him or her to get a breakthrough in their faith walk very fast, because your close ties and deep compassion drive you to see a common outcome. Your faith connected together becomes a strong, reinforced vehicle to carry heavy burdens and to demand miracles. If you have a measure of faith and I have a measure of faith, individually we can each carry a certain load based on our individual faith capacities. However, if we come together and unite our faith measures, then we become a dynamic force against our common foe.

I like to tell people to believe that God considers all prayer petitions. You need to stay in faith until the conclusion comes. You always have at least a fifty percent favor factor leaning your way, and if you add faith, the factor enlarges to one hundred percent.

You have heard this example before, but I will tell it again for the point of illustration. If we compare the operations of faith (things unseen) and the natural (things seen) to a thermostat, we will always find two readings on the thermostat.

One is the current room temperature, and the other indicates the desired room temperature.

Therefore, if the room temperature is seventy-one degrees and you want it to be seventy-five degrees, then you would set the thermostat to seventy-five degrees. When you call for a change in temperature, the wire running from the thermostat to the furnace tells the furnace to bring more heat into the room to reach the desired temperature because the room is not hot enough. You are saying, "The temperature I am currently experiencing is not warm enough; change the condition to match my request."

If the furnace and the thermostat are accurately working, then the furnace engages to generate more heat so that the room can reach the desired temperature. Once the request materializes, the furnace will shut off automatically. If the furnace or the thermostat are not working properly, then either the furnace will run without shutting down, which could lead to mechanical failure and repairs, or the temperature in the room will not match the setting on the thermostat. In other words, it will show a degree that is hotter or colder than the setting. The point is that both elements within the system, the thermostat and the furnace, must work together in order to achieve a common goal, which is to bring more heat into the room to change its current temperature condition. Otherwise, the thermometer reading will be the reality in the room regardless of your comfort or discomfort. You will have to endure the condition of the room until you act to bring change. I heard someone say that, "It's not necessary unless it's necessary." The phrase is a play on words, but you get the meaning!

Now, using the same illustration, the thermometer, for the sake of identification, is your current condition (things seen). It details your actual situation. The thermostat and furnace together take on the persona of faith (things unseen). Faith has the ability to change your current condition through a life of prayer. If you think that a person cannot recover from an illness, then your prayer will reflect that thought. You are saying that the present condition is final and not subject to change. Live with that condition for the rest of your life, because it is your reality. These things happen, and nothing can change.

However, if you think that a person can recover from sickness, you will envision the sickness gone and the person completely healed, and your prayer will agree with the faith picture you captured in your heart for the recovery. Now you are detailing your prayer petition about a temporary condition, because faith for God's reality has come to render your current situation inaccurate and undesirable. You say to God, "I see a better condition in my heart, and here is the requested change I want to bring." The Holy Spirit sees the details, hears the petition and the tenacity of your request, and makes the change to match your faith vision. If you do not see change, then you do not have a clear picture of your petition with a strong yearning to see it happen. Hence, the Holy Spirit does not discern an intense desire from you to warrant a change in your current situation. You could be allowing doubtful distractions to take away your focus and to cloud your clear vision for change. If you can see your answer and believe it, then your faith prayer life can achieve it. Get a vision of recovery for others, and you, too, will recover from your challenges. God finalizes your reality through Jesus your Redeemer! Whose report will you believe? Will you believe your natural, lying eyes, or will you fasten your spiritual eyes on faith? *"For we walk by faith and not by sight"* (*2 Corinthians 5:7).*

Although I had received many teachings on "vision," some things did not click in my mind until after my exposure to the personal testimony of Dr. Cho. Later, I watched Casey Treat faithfully speak the healing Word of God and serve his way into complete restoration from hepatitis C.

Additionally, I saw a specific, detailed desire for change work on two different levels just recently.

First, my youngest sister applied for a job she wanted; so I added my faith to hers. I knew nothing about the job except that she wanted it because she was qualified, had years of experience to fill the position, and needed to change careers due to stress. I prayed for her throughout the interview process. She called back to say that she was not sure if she got the job and that she felt a selection had been made to fill the position. I told her to stay in faith until a final decision was announced. However, she began to allow her feelings and thoughts to overrule her faith request.

We must stay in faith until the final decision comes. God is not solely interested in the result. He is more interested in our transformation through the process rather than the outcome alone. Don't hear me say that He is not concerned about the outcome. After all, He is God. The outcome will be no surprise to Him, but our transformation through the process is fluid as it hinges upon our volition to change.

After my sister refocused her faith and her request of God with my agreement, she found a much better job, one better than she had requested. I do know that the Lord will make it work for her good as a result of her staying in faith!

In John 14:11, Jesus states, *"Believe Me that I am in the Father and the Father in Me, or else believe Me for the sake of the works themselves."* In other words, "If you cannot take My word for it, believe the tangible results that My words produce."

A professional prizefighter with a speech impediment of severe stuttering really does not have to do a lot of talking if he has a history of just knocking folks (TKO) out. Let's face facts. What can he say, or what does he have to say, after knocking someone out? "F-f-fight's over; where's the check?" The result always substantiates the proof.

All those who challenged the many miracles Jesus did had to deal with their unbelief. I mean, if Jesus conversed with them, He did so out of a desire to win them over or to stop them from hindering others from believing for their miracle. What was Jesus going to do: take the miracles back? If a miracle is what you want, you can have one in Jesus. If not, move on! The presence of God is the wrong place for doubting. Miracles are happening in Jesus every day!

Here's one more example. A good friend of mine was experiencing a lack of support from his management at work, causing him to seek new employment. I helped him identify the perfect job with detailed conditions. Then I prayed with him that the job opening would come, and it did within a few weeks. The interviewer, because of prior knowledge, favored him for his plight. He was practically handpicked for his ideal job. He started his new job a few weeks shortly after that prayer. He boldly tells others about his blessing. He left me an excited message referencing our prayer of agreement as the turning point for his new job. We prayed a few days prior to his starting his new job, and he acknowledged God operating in his life! *"The goodness of God leads to repentance" (Romans 2:4)*. God's goodness always yields salvation to those who receive it.

Intercession for others is the way of the kingdom. Jesus lives to make intercession for us. When Job prayed for his friends, his life did a full turn around. *"And the Lord restored Job's losses when he prayed for his friends. Indeed the Lord gave Job twice as much as he had before" (Job 42:10)*. James 5:16 says, *"Pray for one another, that you may be healed."* Praying for one another brings complete restoration through the unity of faith in Jesus.

You have proof that God freely gives His goodness to the just and the unjust alike. If you hold fast to your faith confessions, God will come through for you. Providing for His people is one of God's highest pleasures. He wants the world to know that He is in control. *"Behold, I am the Lord, the God of all flesh. Is there anything too hard for Me" (Jeremiah 32:27)?* In order for the world to get the message, we need only to ask and believe as we pray without ceasing for others! One assurance to getting an answer to prayer is in 1 John 5:14-15.

Now this is the confidence that we have in Him, that if we ask anything according to His will, He hears us. And if we know that He hears us, whatever we ask, we know that we have the petitions that we have asked of Him.

Full acceptance that God is our only source and an undying trust that He both hears and will provide our need solidifies our provision from Him! John 15:7 declares, *"If you abide in me and my words abide in you, you will ask what you desire, and it shall be done for you."* I suspect that many people make innumerable requests to God referencing this particular passage of Scripture. I personally think that the spirit of this Scripture has been reduced in the minds of many to little effect. Let me try again. If you made a request using John 15:7 as your receipt but did not receive your request, then you did not fulfill the first requirement of this Scripture: to abide in Him and let His Word abide in you.

Abiding unequivocally speaks of total surrender versus a heart of stone. You cannot refuse, reject, or ignore God and expect to get His provisions. David attests to this truth in Psalm 51. God desires a *"broken and contrite heart"* (*v. 17*). A sacrifice of this magnitude illustrates a willingness to comply with any and every instruction given by the Father. No refusal lurks in such a heart. Although Jesus walked the earth as a human being, He was simultaneously spiritually divine through obedience. Jesus has power over death and the grave. He took the sting from death and victory from the grave. He is the Lord over all. Hosanna! Glory in the Highest!

Prayer warriors may not see immediate change or experience a visible platform as others do. Nonetheless, they have one of the most important jobs in the kingdom. *"For the weapons of our warfare are not carnal but mighty in God for the pulling down of strongholds" (2 Corinthians 10:4).* The job assignment of prayer is a faith-edged weapon with which intercessors can defeat the enemy. While we all should always pray, thank God for the fervent intercession of our prayer warriors through the gift of intercessory prayer!

Chapter 7

Follow Where God Leads
Inside His Heart

Depth perception is an interesting concept. Although your two eyes see the same thing, each relays information to the brain for processing in a slightly different way. The Father, Son, and Holy Spirit, who are three entities, function as one because they see the exact things and respond in unity with no variance. What one sees and articulates, the others agree to implement.

For example, when you go to the hardware store to purchase a can of special-order paint, the technician must use a base foundation and add a few other mixtures depending on your color request in order to create the exact color you want. Even though various blends having different qualities are added to the base, they have been carefully studied and calculated, ensuring that alliance of their individual properties in reaction to each other is compatible. By adding the mixtures together under the right circumstances, the technician brings to life the color you requested.

Now, if you have a desire for your life that is slightly different from God's desire for your life, you cannot work together with Him for an accomplished end because you are divided. Two contradictory visions are competing one with the other. Jeremiah 29:11 says, *"For I know the thoughts I think towards you, says the Lord, thoughts of peace and not of evil, to give you a future and a hope."* Making any fleshly attempts to outwit God is futile. Any effort to do so is an affront to Him. Face facts: we are incapable of coming up with a better way outside of His way. If we could do so, we would have done so in the Garden.

> *For My thoughts are not your thoughts, nor are your ways My ways, says the Lord. For as the heavens are higher than the earth, so are My ways higher than your ways, and My thoughts than your thoughts. For as the rain comes down, and the snow from heaven, and do not return there, but water the earth, and make it bring forth bud, that it may give seed to the sower and bread to the eater, so shall My word be that goes forth from My mouth; It shall not return to Me void, but it shall accomplish what I please, and it shall prosper in the things for which I sent it.*
> Isaiah 55:8-11

God is making an irrefutable point here; He states, "It was My idea to rain water from the sky on the earth and recycle it, because if I had not, you would need rain daily. You would not like rain daily. So My thoughts and ways, which are superior to yours, dictated that I allow the rain to saturate the earth. Your survival comes from its byproduct carrying reproductive seeds of all sorts. I will not rain daily on one spot [except in Seattle]. Just like I will not recall the rain, I will not recall my Word. It will saturate every situation where it is applied, thereby bringing a reproductive harvest."

In order for a harvest to come, we must consistently follow God's lead. *"How long will you falter between two opinions? If the Lord is God follow Him"* (1 Kings 18:21). Elijah found himself in an impossible situation following God's instructions, but resolution would not come from Elijah. Nonetheless, God brought resolution through Elijah. All Elijah had to do was see the challenge from the eyes of the One who sent him. God sent Elijah for a divine purpose. By following God's instruction without alterations, Elijah set the stage for the Most High to prove Himself. As long as Elijah kept his assignment in mind and his ego in check, God could do miracles. And He did!

While I was in the Marine Corps assigned to the American Consulate in Frankfurt, Germany, I had no idea that my eldest brother, Keith, was in the Air Force two hours away by car in Hahn, Germany. As we communicated, we discovered this proximity. He wanted to see me and I him; so we arranged a meeting. Due to my responsibilities, we decided that he would travel to see me. Prior to our first meeting, he asked if I was saved. I was not sure, because I had never heard the question asked that way. Someone once told me that, if you do not know, you aren't. I was not. Even though I was raised in church as a pastor's kid (PK), I was not familiar with the word "saved." In my earlier years, salvation was simply joining the church. Attending church regularly does not exempt you from your need for salvation. Likewise, singing in the shower does not qualify you to lead praise and worship in front of the entire congregation at your church on Sunday. Please believe me! You really need a personal relationship with Jesus in order to follow where He is leading you.

Well, I became Keith's assignment from the Lord. He drove two hours one way in a no-one-else-wanted-it Datsun 210 of questionable age and ability to pick me up in Frankfurt, and then he drove us back to Hahn to a Bible-teaching church, a four-hour drive in total. I went to church and had to be back the same night. He did the trip in reverse for a total of eight hours of driving in a single day nearly every weekend to get me saved. The Lord told us to win souls at all cost. Keith took God at His word.

Without my brother's obedience to the Word of God and his love for my saved soul, I do not know where I would be. The world was pulling at me and making choosing the right path difficult. Keith stayed the course and counseled me into the hands of God. Now look how God operates. Keith had a family of four. They were living hand-to-mouth. He later told me he went to Family Services every week to get assistance so that they could make ends meet. He was sacrificing the last resources his family had to get me to the house of God.

I thought I would just help him with gas, and I started sending him about one to two hundred dollars a month in addition to tithe. He later told me that the money I sent him saved their lives by allowing them to buy groceries and gas for the car. I did not know his need at the time because he never let on to it. While doing the will of God, we both got our needs met by following biblical principles. God knows exactly what and whom He needs to get His will done! *"Hear instruction and be wise, and do not disdain it" (Proverbs 8:33).* We need only follow His instructions. Sometimes His instructions may not make sense to us, but if we follow them, He will get glory out of our service.

> *But God has chosen the foolish things of the world to put to shame the wise, and God has chosen the weak things of the world to put to shame the things which are mighty; and the base things of the world and the things which are despised God has chosen, and the things which are not, to bring to nothing the things that are, that no flesh should glory in His presence.*
> *1 Corinthians 1:27-29*

God prepared a fish to swallow Jonah in order to convince him to go to Nineveh. Even though, contrary to God's schedule, Jonah delayed his appointment in Nineveh, he was still well within the will of God. The fact that a fish was capable of swallowing Jonah completely without harm indicates that the Almighty was involved and approved Jonah's special mode of transportation.

God used Moses' stick both to split the Red Sea and to strike a rock to provide water for one million people. We know that rock is a substance much more durable and longer lasting than wood. That the very application of wood against the integrity of stone caused a flow of enough water to sustain over one million individuals in the wilderness is nothing shy of miraculous.

Jesus spat on the ground, mixed the wet dirt into putty, and put it on a blind man's eyes to restore his sight. This action, to a person of no faith, is foolishness. The restoration of sight by visiting a doctor with special medical training and certification in the field of vision is acceptable. Crediting a man who just walked into town with a handful of clay and spittle is asking too much. But God can, and He did!

The Apostle Paul's handkerchief served as a point of contact for healing many. I will try a heating pad, ointment, ice treatment, and even injections of Novocain, but the perspiration-stained, unclean handkerchief of a short, round man is not my preferred method of healing. Surely we must give careful consideration to germs and spreading illnesses! Yet Paul's handkerchief traveled around the then civilized world as the agent of change in the lives of many who had a faith need.

After Hezekiah prayed, God instructed Isaiah the prophet to go back to Hezekiah before he left the house and tell him that his life was being lengthened. Isaiah instructed the servants of Hezekiah to put a *"lump of figs" (2 Kings 20:7)* on his boils, and Hezekiah recovered. I know that this instruction seems unusual and awkward to some. However, once God involves Himself in the process, miracles happen.

Right when you think God is going to do something religious to bring change, He uses what is common to man. The Word of God always works. Nevertheless, God expects us to use wisdom, emotion, and our intellect to promote and advance His kingdom. He will take care of the increase. God is ordinarily exceptional, according to 1 Corinthians 1:28-29. He uses the *"base things of the world and the things which are despised God has chosen, and the things which are not, to bring to nothing the things that are, that no flesh should glory in His presence."* God is in a class all by Himself, without exception. His countless miracles attest to His matchlessness.

On June 14, 2008, at 4:16 PM, my family and I received a miracle through following God's instructions. I was driving my family to the grocery store. The road I was driving was very familiar to me, as I frequently traveled it. As we approached a stoplight, a car in front of us stopped at the light. I slowed down as usual, but I sensed a prompting from the Holy Spirit to steer to the left and move forward into the left lane so that we were beside the car stopped at the light. As soon as I followed those instructions, I heard a screeching, rubber-burning slide from a truck behind me as it applied its brakes. That truck, loaded with heavy metal, slid about fifteen feet, right into the spot the Lord had me leave. No cars collided at all. The Lord saved my family from a terrible rear-end accident. Glory to God! Following instructions from the Lord is the difference between life and death!

Knowledge and Understanding

Knowledge and understanding are like smoke and fire. You cannot effectively operate one without the other.

Proverbs 14:33 says, *"Wisdom rests in the heart of him who has understanding, but what is in the heart of fools is made known."* Study and search the Word of God while balancing it with comprehensive sense knowledge (what we hear, see, touch, smell, and taste). *"He who has understanding spares his words, and a man of understanding is of a calm spirit" (Proverbs 17:27).* Know the environment in which you function. Invest time to understand the seasons within (past, present, and future) and your activities while you're doing your life (school, occupation, kids, etc.).

Life is a process with a specific time allotment for each of us. Be sure that you are making the best of your life to impact others to the glory of God. We must strike and maintain a balance of spiritual and sense knowledge throughout our lives. You can generally tell a person's intention based on the focus of his conversation. If you find yourself out of balance, then acquire wisdom, knowledge, and understanding from the Word of God. I believe that the skillful application of sense knowledge could be quite effective, when properly applied, to advance the kingdom of God materially. Proverbs 15:14 states, *"The heart of him who has understanding seeks knowledge."* Knowledge comes from God. He, as the source of all knowledge, loves to hear His children inquiring of Him. Exodus 35:31 says, *"He has filled him with the Spirit of God, in wisdom, and understanding, in knowledge and all manner of workmanship."* When God calls you to a task, He will make you capable of doing it, if you are faithful to Him in all that you do.

Let's examine the career path of a politician. If you want to make a career of politics, then you should understand such things as customs, policy, procedures, pertinent laws, and regulations, as well as how to interact with key officials germane to the effectiveness and efficiency of your position. While word knowledge will help you, your best help will come from your keen understanding of the Word of God and your skillful application of sense knowledge. When you have studied and prepared yourself in the natural realm, God will supplement your efforts with His supernatural power for His divine purpose to reach the masses and spread the gospel. Your directed career path is a vehicle through which God can reach others if you choose to apply yourself.

God's express interest for what He placed inside of you is superseded only by what He expects from you. His return on His investment must yield a profit to advance His divine purpose for your life. If you have a master's degree, that achievement is good, but you should go for a doctorate. Be the best you can be. If a master's degree is not in you, please know that you do have a degree of the Master inside of you. Possessing such a rank, you are without limits if you choose to exercise your gifts and talents all to the glory of God.

If athletes played among themselves without performing for the masses, they would not provide entertainment or experience the fullness of using the talents God placed inside of them. Anointed songsters do not sing to hear themselves. The gift inside of them flows through and beyond them to bless others and bring satisfaction to their souls for properly using their gifts. God placed these various gifts and talents inside each of us to benefit others and to bring glory to His holy name. Guess what? That gift or talent is your ministry! Use it to the glory of God to reach the masses for Jesus. *"And I, if I am lifted up from the earth, will draw all peoples to Myself" (John 12:32).* As you pursue God for your personal mission in life, your focus will help you clearly establish what you were created to do on earth to advance the kingdom of God while continuing Jesus' ministry to win souls!

Desire the Things of God

God materializes His desires through us. Ezekiel 36:26 says, *"I will give you a new heart and put a new spirit within you; I will take the heart of stone out of your flesh and give you a heart of flesh."* I believe that we have desires that lay dormant in our hearts until we dare to dream. God is able to do all things. When we believe He can and act on that belief, God is obligated to fulfill our desires that bring glory to His name. While He can physically give us a new heart because He is God, I think that this Scripture speaks to our desires instead. When our heart desires the things of God, bringing those desires to pass gives Him pleasure. What are your desires?

In addition to giving us new desires, God is committed to helping us make them happen. Then He said, *"I will put My spirit within you and cause you to walk in My statutes, and you will keep My judgments and do them" (Ezekiel 36:27).* He will put His character, strength of mind, and determination within us to help us fulfill the new desires He gives us. In other words, God will set us up for success and then help us succeed! As we know that the new desires He gives us will be pure in nature, we cannot lose, because our desires came from God. Set your affections on the things of God.

> *If then you were risen with Christ, seek those things which are above, where Christ is, sitting at the right hand of God. Set your mind on the things above, not on things on earth. For you died, and your life is hidden with Christ in God.*
> *Colossians 3:1-3*

Jesus showed us how to accomplish what we so often quote. Scripture clearly challenges us to make the transition from earth to heaven while on earth. Yes, we need water, food, and shelter, but these daily essentials should not take first place over the things of God. I am not suggesting that we should do without these things or even fail to plan such provisions. But we should not allow our daily thought process to be burdened with such thoughts. The Bible tells us that God is aware of our daily needs and has already provided them. We need to believe, trust, and receive His provisions. Settle your mind to know that God is bigger than a Grand Slam breakfast or a Happy Meal. I know that this kind of faith is easy for a person who has an abundant supply of daily essentials. For those who do not have daily essentials, this belief can present challenging opportunities. However, I believe that the same principle applies. Believe that God can supply your needs, trust Him to do so of His own choosing, and receive provision by faith. Philippians 4:19 declares, *"And my God shall supply all your need, according to His riches in glory by Christ Jesus."* If you believe what you just now read, then move your feet toward your provisions. In other words, get busy doing something that will allow God to open doors of opportunities to meet your needs.

In 1991, I experienced not having enough resources and food for a few days on my first big job in Boston, Massachusetts. I discovered that the bank did not give me enough money to cover the extra checks I had left over. Simply put, I overextended my resources while trying to impress others. During this time, most of my friends had retired or were transitioning from the military. I was in transition without adequate resources. We were all invincible, especially me, the country boy unfamiliar with how things work in the city. Survival of the fittest was in full play. The others had their families nearby for support. Nonetheless, I overextended my resources and quickly bottomed out. I needed help, but I was too proud to ask my parents, friends, or anyone else. I was in an embarrassing situation and silenced by shame and lack. I had to trust God as my source for five reasons:

1. I had no personal means by which to sustain myself.
2. I was buried in debt.

3. I was too embarrassed to ask for assistance because of my lack of stewardship.
4. I did not want to suffer embarrassment from being exposed.
5. I was exhausted, weary from worrying, and deeply concerned about my image.

After adding up my debt and recognizing my inability to help myself, I turned my lack into a spiritual quest. I had been hearing about fasting, and I thought that now was a good time to try, as I had no food. I went on a three-day fast. After all, I had nothing to lose and everything to gain. Well, after a few days, God fixed my lack through my acquaintance with a coworker who had been hired same time as I was. G. Robert was married, and his wife, Joyce, had a miracle-working kitchen ministry accompanied by fresh aromas and hunger-healing vitals. Of course, after three days of famine in my camp, a slice of bread with butter would have surpassed the daily-manna-from-heaven miracle in the Bible. Anyway, Robert and Joyce invited me over for the first of many visits. The first visit was for a full weekend. We really did not know each other, but an unspoken affinity was between us. They were big-hearted people. During our first visit over the weekend, three distinct revelations surfaced during our get-to-know-each-other, warm-up conversation. They loved to cook and had no live-in kids. I loved to eat, and I had not eaten for three days.

The feast was on! They always had the challenge of leftover meals to deal with prior to my visits. I brought resolution. I'm a firm believer that, if we solve problems for others, our compensation should parallel the solution. I accepted my reward in the form of "all-I-could-eat- payments." They were never late on their payments. I was never late receiving them. Oh, happy day!

This season in my life may seem like a small provision to those who have, but to those who have not: point made. Go for God with all that is within you, and He will embrace you into His courts of provision where He has more than enough. Just follow His instructions!

Knowing that you received instructions from God takes faith, because normally the instructions will have you do something that you would not otherwise do. Likewise, developing the right character traits while you fulfill those instructions takes a measure of faith.

> *But also for this very reason, giving all diligence, add to your faith virtue, to virtue knowledge, to knowledge self-control, to self-control perseverance, to perseverance godliness, to godliness brotherly kindness, and to brotherly kindness love.*
>
> *2 Peter 1:5-7*

As these traits become more visible in your life, instructions from God become clearer and more frequent. In effect, you have adjusted your character to the frequency through which God transmits heavenly information. Hearing instructions from God, at this point, is clear, exciting, and familiar!

Mary told those at the wedding to follow Jesus' every instruction. When they did, He turned water to fine wine. Jesus instructed Peter to come out of the boat onto the water. He instructed the disciples to go into the entire world preaching the gospel. He instructed the disciples to sit the multitude down in an organized manner as he fed them from a few fishes and several loaves of bread. He instructed the sea and the waves to be still, and they obeyed, thereby changing the hostile environment that brought fear to many people. Always remember that a single phrase or word of instruction from God will transform your life from lack to plenty if you follow it!

Chapter 8

Better to Obey
Listen; Then Do It!

The highest form of recognizing God is obeying Him with absolute trust. We prove our surrender to Him by spontaneously acting out the level of instructions He communicates to us without reservation. Jeremiah 29:11 reads, *"For I know the thoughts I think towards you, says the Lord, thoughts of peace and not of evil, to give you a future and a hope."* We have to accept that God's intent for our life is always better than our own. Therefore, be quick to obey His instructions.

Picture yourself as the first officer of an aircraft that is on approach for landing when the captain directs you to lower the landing gear. You decide to disregard the captain's instructions, opting to slow down instead. By your decision, you will cause the aircraft to respond. However, the response you created out of disobedience did not address the captain's command. By obeying the instructions given to you as an obedient first officer, you would have corrected the aircraft's position and avoided future unnecessary adjustments. Had you lowered the landing gear, the visual experience the captain encountered, causing him to issue his initial command would have been a learning opportunity for you. That kind of opportunity is why he sits on the left and you sit on the right. I have been told by a pilot friend of mine that the first officer can fly the aircraft just as well as the captain. While this statement is true, the captain has complete authority to oversee the overall welfare of the aircraft and its cargo. Even though each pilot learns to operate the aircraft from a standard operating procedure manual, each pilot will have specific idiosyncrasies when he is in full charge of the aircraft. In like manner, we must obey God equally. We need only follow His instructions, because He knows the beginning and the end.

Nehemiah understood the principle of everyone working in his or her place based on his or her various talents. Nehemiah's desire to rebuild the wall in the allotted time demanded that he strategically deploy families according to their abilities. As they focused on their work zones, they quickly repaired the wall in unity. Imagine if all of the families repairing the wall of Jerusalem took time away from their places to see how others were doing. The wall would still be in disrepair. We tend to critique and judge the works of others. We should never allow or be led to believe that our way is better than God's assignment for others. Encourage, support, and pray for others where you can, as long as the kingdom of God is growing followed by miracles, signs, and wonders that lead to winning souls. Do not judge, interfere, or impede the fresh movement of God because of your preference, inclination, or bias. Everyone has his or her season of shining for God on center stage. Do not interfere with someone's season of obedience to God on center stage.

One of the most precious gifts we can give in return for all God has done for us is to live a life of obedience unto Him. He gave us the best gift He could give in Jesus. While we cannot give a better gift than His, He expects us to give our best gift: our lives in the form of obedience with service and gratitude, living our lives as thanks. We tend to equal a gift given to us by others to show our gratefulness. Following this line of thinking, we should live our lives with gratefulness for the gift our Lord has given to us. Live your life with gratitude through obedience as a thank-you to Jesus for all that He did for us!

God requires our obedience so that our lives will touch the lives of others. By obeying, we affect the kingdom of God on earth as it is in heaven. The supreme will of God is for all of us to obey Him by following the example of Jesus. Let's note this location in the eternal process of being a member of the divine family. A part of sustaining and advancing everything that Jesus accomplished prior to His ascension comes from our obedience to God. Our observed obedience to God is paramount to the well-being and growth of His family. The body of Christ exists to share the Good News of the gospel to every nation, people, and tongue while expressing God's undying and forgiving love unto the salvation of all. Our mandate is to carry out the works of ministry and to take dominion until Jesus returns.

Reexamine the work of the cross from the view of our Lord once again. The level of committed obedience Jesus displayed for us is uniquely unparalleled in practice. While sacrifices for the preservation of life have been recorded, few have been acknowledged within the scope of divinity, and without reservation, none has accomplished the works of the cross. The Father and the Son introduce the highest form of obedience, sacrifice, and eternal love.

For scarcely for a righteous man will one die; yet perhaps for a good man someone would even dare to die. But God demonstrates His own love toward us, in that while we were still sinners, Christ died for us.

Romans 5:7-8

Jesus Christ gives the best example of obedience even unto death. *"Looking unto Jesus, the author and finisher of our faith, who for the joy set before Him endured the cross, despising the shame" (Hebrews 12:2)*. Our Lord submitted to the redemptive suffering and sacrifice required to remedy the woes of man through the works of the cross. In His obedience to the Father and triune Godhead since the foundation of the world, Jesus clearly communicated the necessity, importance, and consequence of His obedient sacrifice.

Always remember that, while obedience to the will of God may be uncomfortable to you for a moment, someone is waiting for the open door that you will provide through that same obedient sacrifice. I will remind you that this is your *"reasonable service" (Romans 12:1)*. In other words, if you do, then someone else will. If you obey God, then others will get blessed in the process. The principle is that simple. The foundational question in this book is: why does man struggle to develop and maintain a significant relationship with God? One answer to the question is that we fail to obey the will of God. Purposing to live valiantly would cure such a struggle. We have within our own ability, through faith, the very means to end our struggle to establish and maintain a sincere, meaningful relationship with God. Obedience is the key to living a valiant life for Christ.

Our Lord had a clear and vivid perspective for the outcome of His obedience. Consequently, He was willing to perform this historically redemptive event. Therefore, Hebrews 12:2 affirms, *"Who for the joy set before Him endured the cross, despising the shame."* Let's not forget that Jesus is the second part of the triune deity of God: God the Father (Creator), God the Son (Jesus), and God the Holy Spirit. As God the Son, Jesus was deeply concerned to the point of releasing bloodlike perspiration in the Garden of Gethsemane as He spoke to the Father. However, after the fall the whole of man had no other way to effect regeneration, becoming one with

Almighty God. Our Jesus was obedient unto His death by humbling Himself to pay the lofty price required as payment for the fall of man. He made a way for everyone, regardless of race, creed, color or gender, etc. What a Savior!

We find a good example of hearing followed by obedience in 1 Samuel 16. Sometimes obeying God will require us to set aside a qualified emotion. Samuel illustrates this example as he mourns Saul's death. Saul had the assignment to obliterate the entire lineage of Amalek. Saul disobeyed God's instructions to destroy Amalek. As a result, the Lord rejected him as king. While Samuel did not agree with Saul's action, he valued the loss of what could have been had Saul only obeyed God. God recognized Samuel's demeanor; however, the business of appointing the next obedient king took precedence. In verse 1, God commissions Samuel to prepare for a journey to Jesse so that he could anoint the next king. Samuel, despite his mourning Saul's rejection, takes the journey and obeys God. Because of his obedience, the presence of God rested with Samuel to ensure that he did not anoint the wrong candidate. Through the divine wisdom of God, Samuel was able to discern who among the sons of Jesse would be the next king of Israel. God's presence gave Samuel patience, clarity, wisdom, and peace to endure the interviewing process to get to David. You need the presence of God and the boundless attributes that accompany Him in every aspect of your life. Even though Samuel had a deep respect for Saul as king, he valued his obedience to the will and presence of God more.

God loves to reward those of us who follow His instructions, because our obedience proves without a doubt His dominion rule. Every instruction from God has a purpose. When we do what God asks of us, we bring glory to Him. As a reward, He always reminds us of our promised inheritance. *"But my servant Caleb, because he has a different spirit in him and has followed Me fully, I will bring into the land where he went, and his descendants shall inherit it" (Numbers 14:24).*

God values our obedience to Him so highly that any act of defiance or noncompliance on our part displays the most horrid rebellious act towards our God in which we could engage! When God communicates to us His will, we deeply insult Him when we, the creation, entertain a wayward thought contrary to His sovereign and self-sustaining communication. God's words are so full of life that when He speaks, His word is like a seed, which contains everything needed to produce an orchard except for soil and water. Instruction from God is likewise. When we hear it and allow it into our hearts, our hearts become the soil. As we activate faith to believe it, our faith serves as water bringing nutrients to the soil. Because our words spoken in faith designate an expected value to what we believe God will do, He is obligated to fulfill our intense expectation as we live in full faith. *"Has the Lord as great delight in burnt offerings and sacrifices, as in obeying the voice of the Lord? Behold, to obey is better than sacrifice, and to heed than the fat of rams" (1 Samuel 15:22).* Everything God has done, is doing, and will do for us derives from His best resources. *"If you are willing and obedient, you shall eat the good of the land" (Isaiah 1:19).*

Wait a Minute

Wait on God. Do not get ahead of Him. Many times, we ask God for something and shortly set our faith to receive it. The balance of our time is in His capable hands; He prefers not to operate on our timetable. However, He does meet our needs on time. God knows everything that we need. Obeying God synchronizes our agenda to His. Once synchronized to the Father, we find our urgency and haste dissipating. Because He is in control of our situations, we should not hinder progress by interfering with His divine process. Just wait on Him to lead, and then obey His instructions.

Complete Assurance

You have to know for yourself who God is and what He means to you. Knowing this truth without reservation empowers you to endure life's challenges and to enter your place of rest, where God places peace all around you and resources to fulfill your destiny within your reach. No matter how tough life gets or what it throws at you, never give up on God, because the balance of your time belongs to Him. God is right there with you, revealing His provisions in small but noticeable ways. *"Be still and know that I am God" (Psalm 46:10).*

When you are confident about your ability to perform a task, but then find opposition, you do not need to engage in an altercation with anyone over the facts. When the time comes to act, you obey, stay calm and just do what you should. The very fact that you acted from obedience speaks volumes. God is always speaking, but He whispers in a *"still small voice" (1 King 19:12).* He is confident that He can deliver you from every situation. You need to have the same confidence in Him, and follow the whisper. Swallow your pride, and submit. After all, He is omniscient, omnipotent, and omnipresent. He is everything! Do not be offended. Be glad that He is allowing you to participate and offering you help beyond your limitation. I tell my kids all the time, "Do not run from help; run to it!" You will be glad of help when your swollen pride disappears.

I can remember driving in a taxi towards 58 Rue Leboite, the street in Paris on which the American Embassy is located. This particular night, the city was celebrating a holiday by setting off lots of fireworks and escorting dignitaries all around. The nonstop sirens and flashing lights confirmed that the main streets in the business district were closed. I could not get through the traffic in the taxi, and I hardly knew my way well enough to walk. Because I needed to be at the embassy for work, I opted to walk. I took twenty-five minutes to reach my destination, only because I followed the whisper of the Holy Spirit. He led me with sure confidence right to the front door of the embassy, bypassing many security checkpoints, unstopped. I never had to show my identification a single time until I arrived at the embassy. What we can do with what God knows if we listen and confidently trust His provisions is amazing!

My son got a pair of tennis shoes with pop-out wheels like skates in the heels that enable him to roll. He could not wait to try them. This pressing desire caused him to ask me to move the car from the garage so that he could break the shoe in. It was very cold, and I did not want to move from my very comfortable spot. So his first request was for me simply to move the car. I replied, "No way!" Five minutes later, his second attempt took a completely new approach that disarmed me. He simply thanked me for moving the car. I sat up in complete surprise at this new tactic, puzzled as to what his angle was. He must have seen daylight. I admit that his unwavering confidence in getting his request cause my heart to soften. He kept busy with a few other things, and about five minutes later, he struck gold. My son asked on the third attempt, "About what time are you going to move the car from the garage so that I could try my new shoes, Dad?" I immediately got up and moved the car. He met me at the door and said, "I knew it! THANKS, Dad!"

Press On

Everything that God has for you does not always come easy. God has labeled some of His blessings for you "time sensitive." In other words, you have to endure the journey with God through the valleys and peaks in your life until you get to your appointed time. *"Then the Lord appointed a set time, saying, 'Tomorrow the Lord will do this thing in the land'" (Exodus 9:5).* I warn you that, when your time comes, it ushers in showered seasons of special consideration and allowances from God that will make others notice you for the created purpose to which the Lord has called you. In this season of your life, God rewards you by rescinding rules, shattering time limitations, and suspending natural impossibilities.

Prior to the horrible attack on our financial district in Manhattan, I had a great career, but I felt underutilized. For example, a few days after the dreadful September 11 terrorist attack on our country, I was on my way to Montana to implement and assess new security measures at various regional airports. I did not want to be in Montana, but I followed my supervisor's instructions in obedience, serving man as unto the Lord. Upon returning to my office, I was unexpectedly called up to the regional manager, who told me to contact the director of the Federal Air Marshal Service immediately. I did. After a very brief conversation with him (situation bearing), I flew to Atlantic City, New Jersey for a special meeting with him. While there for almost thirty days, I received instructions to return to Seattle and establish a District Field Office for the Federal Air Marshal Service; I had very little guidance, aside from being told to press on and get the job done. They were in for an experience and just did not know it. God had a plan! Well, I flew back to Seattle and built the office. Within ninety days, the contemporary, state-of-the-art facility was operational. The Director personally conducted the dedication of the facility in disbelief that it had been finished with excellence. Many wanted to do what I did and would have jumped at the opportunity. God predetermined that my appointed time had come and favored me as someone capable of accomplishing the assignment for such a time. He gave me center stage in my season to declare His awesome power. When I was at a low point, buried in frustration from underutilization, God showed Himself strong in me to address a dire need of the nation. I promise you that He got a lot of praise and glory out of my unique and highly favored opportunity! My office, the first of its kind in the nation, came to completion ahead of schedule and under budget, and it served as a model for other upcoming offices around the country. The director was so impressed with the advanced technological capabilities within the office that he designated it the backup to the national headquarters facility. The Lord reestablished His name and His power in the eyes of those who witnessed our facility. Glory to the Most High God!

Prior to building and managing this new facility with thousands of square footage and hundreds of full-time employees, I had applied for a supervisor's position. My supervisor and others who evaluated me thought I was not ready for leadership because I was too kind. They overlooked my hardworking, dependable, and knowledgeable qualities to discredit me with being too nice. How about that disqualifier? The arrival of a leader who would care about his followers and get the job done was an obvious threat that met low tolerance. God help our workforce!

Well, at the age of forty-four, after being promoted into executive management following September 11, I resigned with twenty-three years of excellent service at the pinnacle of my career as a productive leader, having accomplished more than those who commented on my qualifications. God gave me my season to showcase what He had deposited inside of me. He exposed my abilities to the others by setting me center stage in the heat of the battle to bring resolution to a major problem. He touched the king's heart in my favor. The king in this situation was the director of the Federal Air Marshal Service.

Mighty warrior
Dressed for battle,
Holy Lord of all is He.
Commander-in-Chief,
Bring us to attention;
Lead us into battle
To crush the enemy.

                                    Debbye Graafsma[18]

What God has for you is for you. No one can substitute for you, steal away your opportunity, or stop you from getting into this place except YOU. So press on into your appointed time. The Lord is preparing your season right now. Press on, and press in to all God has for you! Hallelujah!

Choose to Serve

Romans 12:1 says, *"I beseech you therefore, brethren, by the mercies of God, that you present your bodies a living sacrifice, holy, acceptable to God, which is your reasonable service."* Voluntarily serve God. The army of God does not consist of drafted men and women unwillingly ordered into service. God never owned a slave. He does not force us to do anything against our will.

All who desire to follow Jesus are free to come. *"Whoever desires to come after Me, let him deny himself, and take up his cross, and follow Me" (Mark 8:34).* That invitation from our Lord is very broad. Who is inclusive and receptive to everyone? Yes! If you are willing to live a life of committed sacrifice, then follow Jesus. He consistently asks for volunteers. He invites us to the enjoyment of a privileged life. He does not call us to forced labor, picking cotton or working in sweat shops, but lovingly appeals as a Father to His children to partake of all He has to give. I sincerely believe that God wants us to sit down and deeply consider

His goodness toward us in the process of life. He really is good to us. In order to be exempt from this consideration, ask yourself, "Has God done anything for me lately?" Keep in mind that the very air you breathe belongs to Him. If He has not done anything for you, then you are exempted from His provisions. If He has, then take a little time to thank Him for whatever comes to your recollection. If you really get down to business, you could take the rest of your life just thanking Him for where you are right now. No matter what you think about your current situation, it could be worse. God has preserved you through everything. We owe Him our gratitude and worship!

Chapter 9

Disrespect from Disobedience
Return to Me

Submitting to God's authority or opposing Him are simple acts of will. I am amazed, but nonetheless grateful, at how God extends grace to those who disrespect Him through disobedience. How can we allow others or ourselves to get to the place where continuing our daily reliance on the goodness of God through His grace becomes nonessential? I pray that we choose to stand and walk close to our Lord and never lose sight of His kindness towards us.

Any time a church leader has to deal with a believer who has become uncaring, stubborn, or headstrong in submission, the leader bears an unnecessary burden. This behavior brings unfaithfulness or disrespect. Many examples in Scripture prove that such behavior towards the Almighty stems from vanity. Hebrews 10:30-31 asserts, *"'Vengeance is Mine, I will repay, says the Lord.' It is a fearful thing to fall into the hands of the living God."*

Israel's King Ahaz found himself in a sullen disposition when he decided to sever his affiliation with the Lord. Due to the king's state of emotion, he actually believed that the gods of the king of Syria championed his cause in the place of the God of Israel. My close relationship with God is too precious for me to risk losing at any cost. I guess that, when we are absorbed in ourselves, we very easily lose touch with more important things. I mean, if I am the most important thing to me, then nothing else matters. Because he focused on himself, the king lost sight of the most important relationship in his life. A simple review from his scribes would have revealed the favor Israel enjoyed by following God. He should have called upon his scribes to read the records to remind him of the goodness of God.

Ahaz wrote a decree to shut off access to the house of God for worship. He did so under misguided pretenses. His fatal decision impacted the entire nation of Israel and the king.

> *And if it seems evil to you to serve the Lord, choose for yourselves this day whom you will serve, whether the gods which your fathers served that were on the other side of the River, or the gods of the Amorites, in whose land you dwell. But as for me and my house, we will serve the Lord.*
>
> *Joshua 24:15*

Do not let anyone decide your personal level of devotion and worship to God. You have the right to worship the Almighty without restraint. Exercise your right daily.

King Ahaz began to sacrifice to the pagan gods and to worship them, even though God's command was clear that *"you shall have no other gods before me" (Exodus 20:3)*. Be very careful to observe the Word of God. The supposition here is that we take time to study and know the Word. Subsequently, King Ahaz deliberately offended and insulted the Lord by acknowledging other gods. *"And in every single city of Judah he made high places to burn incense to other gods, and provoked to anger the Lord God of his fathers"* (2

Chronicles 28:25). Ahaz surrendered to the stress brought on through leadership and became very unfaithful to God. He could not endure his circumstances, and so he quit fighting. Because of his decision to turn away from God, King Ahaz died out of the will of God, empty and unfulfilled.

Let's look at King Saul. Saul did not obey when God instructed him to destroy Amalek and take nothing from the spoils because Amalek had previously ambushed the nation of Israel as they left Egypt. Saul sidestepped his mission and decided to promote his own agenda rooted in ambition. He spared King Agag and some of his best livestock in direct disobedience to God. Subsequently, he lost his leadership and influence for a simple act of insubordination. Now, you might think that a leader such as Saul was wise to provide for the welfare of his army. After all, they had to travel quickly to position themselves to engage the battle. Surely an army, if properly rested and nourished, can quickly show a speedy recovery after such an engagement with the enemy. Please contemplate the error of Saul's action and understand that any act of disobedience towards God is repulsive to Him. *"For rebellion is as the sin of witchcraft, and stubbornness is as iniquity and idolatry" (1 Samuel 15:23).*

The Spirit of Amalek

Saul failed miserably by not following God's order to obliterate Amalek. Behind every act of man, a corresponding spirit bears influence either for good or for evil. Obviously, God decided that Amalek's ambush on Israel was not in the best interest of either nation, especially Israel. God had heard the desperate cries of Israel, and He decided that He wanted them to be free to worship and serve Him in the wilderness. He desired to have an intense relationship with them and to show them favor for crying out to Him even under bondage.

Your wilderness or dry land should produce a hunger for the presence of God.

Using Israel as an example, we know that God does hear us no matter where we are, and He will answer our every petition that promotes His kingdom's campaign to win souls. God knew that He had to sever the leadership rule Egypt had over Israel in order for His divine purpose to have priority in Israel's lives. God would not permit the likes of Amalek to dismantle the love He wanted to shower down on Israel as He rescued them from Egypt's bondage. He watched over His children with a keen eye to place them under His graceful provision. To this day, we are still dealing with the consequences of Saul's disobedience to a direct order from God to destroy Amalek.

We see another act of disobedience to God in 2 Chronicles 35:20-24. Josiah, the king of Israel, sincerely observed Passover to the level of Samuel the prophet. From the time of Samuel until Josiah, Israel observed Passover at various levels of devotion. In those days, the king's relationship with God determined the level of celebration for Passover. God had highly blessed the nation of Israel. Josiah kept the Passover with intense devotion to the things of God for eighteen consecutive years. However, he failed to yield to instructions from God, which came by way of an equal peer, King Necho of Egypt.

> *I have not come against you this day, but against the house with which I have war; for God commanded me to make haste, Refrain from meddling with God, who is with me, lest He destroy you.*
> *2 Chronicles 35:21*

Josiah was determined to set the battle with Necho. But raging against the counsel of God is a dangerous thing to do. Sometimes, when we are not careful to recognize God in various activities, we tend to make a decision based on how God previously responded to us instead of experiencing a fresh new move or direction. Now, here comes Necho with instructions from God to battle and defeat Carchemish. Please do not miss this unspoken cue for Josiah. God did not inform Josiah of this battle between the king of Egypt and Carchemish prior to Necho showing up at the Euphrates River to set the battle.

Take note. Regardless of the variety of activities, special programs, and events taking place in your proximity, you must be very careful of your involvement and participation with them. Unless God authorizes you to participate or releases favor for you to align yourself with what He is doing in another location, even if it's in your backyard, stand still and watch His salvation at work. Learn from it. You may not understand what is taking place. Nonetheless, you are not supposed to run everywhere and be a part of everything God is doing. For us to stay in our own lane and focus on our individual task is paramount. All authority belongs to God, and He alone directs the tempo and determines the rate of progress in each task He assigns.

A man and his daughter took a night walk under a star-bright sky. The little girl looked up into the vault of heaven, so thickly studded with the twinkle of the orbs, and said, "Let's count them Papa." Beginning with one, she counted five and ten and twenty and thirty and forty and fifty and up to one hundred, and then one hundred and twenty-six. She said, "Papa, I am tired; there are one hundred and twenty-six stars. I did not know there were so many." Astronomers estimate that the Milky Way alone has about one hundred thousand million stars. Outside that number are millions upon millions of other galaxies also! You might think that counting the drops of water in the sea or grains of sands on the seashores would be better. Nonetheless, God's mercies and thoughts of you exceed the total sum of all stars in the heavens and drops of waters into the sea and grains of sands on the seashores, for they are innumerable. When you really think about His level of devotion, what reason, if any, justifies insolence and rebellion against God? Life is so much better when we obey and prefer His desire to our own. In God is no start or finish. We would be wise to align our lives to His service. Just as He gave His Son's life for us, we should dedicate our lives to Him.

The Importance of Light

God is a holy and righteous God. The Bible declares in 1 John 1:5 that *"God is light and in Him is no darkness at all."* None! His sovereign cry is that we, as royal descendants, become holy even as He is holy. The very fact that God demands holiness and righteousness insists that some oppose His demand. The opposite of holiness and righteousness is disobedience and sin. To get to the place God has for us, we need to implement a lifestyle of obeying God and His words. In His eyes, nothing is better. In other words, do not give Him what you think He wants. Do what He has already instructed you to do, and He will get the results He wants.

John 3:19 says, *"Men loved darkness rather than light, because their deeds were evil."* Because of our sin nature, for man to outwit a holy and pure God is impossible. God created man, a fact which bears in and of itself the posture of insufficiency. Never will man, as the creation, rise above his Creator, who exacts a penalty for disobedience. When we exercise the free volition our Creator has granted to us to thumb our noses at Him or flagrantly disregard His instructions, we enter an arena God identifies as sin. *"For the wages of sin is death; but the gift of God is eternal life through Jesus Christ our Lord" (Romans 6:23).* Man received exoneration from the penalty and stain of sin through the light of Jesus. Jesus paid the sin debt in total. But beyond the work of the cross is an expected requirement for man; man must reconcile his sin nature dead by the work accomplished on the cross of Jesus. Once accepted, the cross provides a foundation to live a new life in God. When we submit to the will of God, He is sure to promote us as available vessels to carry out His divine purpose for our lives. Obedience opens the door for grace. The grace of God hides the old, blemished life we had without God.

> *Therefore, as through one man's offense [disobedience] judgment came to all men, resulting in condemnation, even so through one Man's righteous act [obedience] the free gift came to all men, resulting in justification of life.*
> *Romans 5:18*

Now that we understand the significance between obedience and disobedience to God, we see how God applied unending grace to the likes of the nation of Israel, Jonah, Moses, Miriam, Aaron, David, and Paul, etc. I hesitate listing others, as you and I do periodically qualify among those listed. Glory to God for His amazing grace!

Chapter 10

The Pretender
Misrepresenting God

As children of the Most High, we must live with distinction among others who do not confess Him. Our decorum should attract others to Him and make us stand out as an illustration of a good life in Jesus. Matthew 5:14 says, *"You are the light of the world. A city that is set on a hill cannot be hidden."* We are obligated to a life of holiness that is unadulterated, not tucked away for fear of not fitting. We need to model modest behavior and self-control, convincing others to live for Jesus. We should not become pretenders of God while assimilating to fit the standards of the world.

Too often, we shirk our rightful places because of our own inability to deal with our holy heritage. Luke 16:8 explains, *"For the sons of this world are more shrewd in their generation than the sons of light."* Unbelievers are cleverly more articulate concerning the justification of their life choices than most believers. They are content because no one has convinced them otherwise. If they can be that bold in their unbelief, ultimately resulting in eternal separation, believers should be encouraged to promote holiness.

At the same time, we should strike a balance. *"Behold I send you out as sheep in the midst of wolves. Therefore be wise as serpents and harmless as doves" (Matthew 10:16).* If you are not careful, you may win arguments concerning right and wrong. What good is winning the argument but losing an opportunity to win a soul into the kingdom?

We are of the Father, but He is not of us. While we are required to live a life acceptable unto holiness to lead others to Christ, we are only the messengers and not the source. I will say this: we are to be very careful in our witness not to position ourselves or allow others to position us in a role we cannot fill. Jesus is Savior; we are receivers of His salvation. Let no one cause you to think or believe otherwise. Our persons and all of our possessions belong to Him alone. Therefore, the need to personally attain deity or a glorified posture should never arise within us. All glory and honor belong to God.

> You alone are Holy,
> You alone are Almighty God.
> You alone are worthy.
> Jesus, we lift You up.
> You are the God of creation,
> Lord over everything.
> All glory and honor we give You,
> My God, You alone.
>
> Kim Wesolek[19]

Self-glorification or aggrandizement is such a deadly disposition in the family of God. Isaiah 42:8 decrees, *"I am the Lord, that is My name; And My glory I will not give to another, nor My praise to carved images."* Our Father is very careful to establish and protect the boundaries of His deity. When the creature believes that it is equal to or better than the Creator, something unusual occurs. When Eve believed she could be as knowledgeable as God by eating the fruit in the Garden (Genesis 3:6), something unusual occurred. When Lucifer subscribed to be as God in the heavens (Isaiah 14:12-15), something unusual occurred. Every time a creature of God positions itself to be God, something unusual happens. God is obliged by His own holiness to preserve dominion over the universe. We can never afford to be led into the pretentiousness of being God.

In 2 Chronicles 26, we find an example of a direct misrepresentation of God. King Uzziah was a God-fearing man. He ruled his nation with a heart for God. God made him prosperous in all that he did. The people loved him because he protected them and defended the nation from various enemies. Uzziah prepared special weaponry and engineered mechanical devices from the strategies of his leaders. He became so famous that his fame spread from Jerusalem to Egypt. Many paid tribute to him, for his fame stretched greatly throughout the land.

The king began to glorify himself. *"But when he was strong his heart lifted up, to his destruction, for he transgressed against the Lord his God by entering the temple of the Lord to burn incense on the altar of incense" (v. 16).* This burning of incense was a priestly function. Uzziah was a king, not a priest. He got out of his lane and took on a responsibility not assigned to him. Be very careful both to know your office of responsibility and not to step into someone else's role. By entering the temple to burn incense, Uzziah misrepresented God. Something unusual was about to happen.

Azariah the priest challenged Uzziah and instructed him to get out of the sanctuary (vv. 17-18). Notice that the challenge to the king came from the priest, who holds a parallel leadership role. The king is accountable for the nation, while the priest is accountable for the sanctuary. Inside the domain of their respective offices, they are second only to God.

Anytime misrepresentation of God's holiness occurs, He is obligated to address the very act. The response from God becomes a matter of record for all others to learn in order to prevent others from making the same mistake. Uzziah forgot where he was in the heat of anger, and God reminded him by striking him with leprosy on his forehead (v. 19). Uzziah stayed a leper for the remainder of his days, isolated and cut off from the house of the Lord (v. 21).

Another example of misrepresentation is in the book of Acts, chapter 5. Ananias and his wife Sapphira hid income from a real estate deal they made, or so they thought, and they lied to Peter concerning the sum of money in their possession. Immediately, the Holy Spirit prompted Peter to address the issue. After Peter challenged Ananias for his deception, Ananias fell down and breathed his last breath (vv. 4-5). This death was the first time in the New Testament where God meted out this level of punishment. I believe that God was establishing His guidelines for how the new church would operate, and He decided to publish His guidelines in the minds and hearts of the people.

Notice how fear came upon all those who heard these things (v. 5). No one should have been in any doubt as to the recompense for attempting to deceive the Lord. No one sang funeral songs like *Nearer my God to Thee* or *In the Sweet Bye and Bye* or prayed. They just picked Ananias up, took him out, dug a hole, and buried him (v. 6).

Now one verse later, in walked Sapphira, unaware that her deceptive husband had died and was lying in a grave out back (v. 7). Peter questioned her concerning the truth. Oh, yes she did! She stuck to her lie, too (vv. 8-9). Well, by the time she fell dead, in walked the men who had just buried her husband. They had to make another trip back out to the graveyard to bury her by her deceptive husband (vv. 9-10).

> *Great fear [reverence and respect for the things of God] came upon the church and those who heard. And through the hands of the Apostles many signs and wonders were done among the people.*
> Acts 5:11-12

I believe that if God had looked away from the actions of Ananias and Sapphira, verse 12 would not exist in the Bible, because the people would not be able to receive for having a heart of stone. Their hearts were softened and turned towards God after hearing how He dealt with Ananias and Sapphira.

Instruments of God

We are God's own handiwork. We are nothing without Him. As His own handiwork, we are obliged to do His will when and as He instructs.

> *And do not present your members as instruments of unrighteousness to sin, but present yourselves to God as being alive from the dead, and your members as instruments of righteousness to God.*
> Romans 6:13

Because God is the source of our lives, we operate under His righteousness through Christ Jesus according to our faith in Him. Being made righteous through Him, we are no longer our own. He gave us a new identity through the divine works of the cross. Therefore, all that we are and ever will be belongs to His service. God has established a clear order of dominion on the earth and in heaven with specific insight from His eternal thoughts.

> *Shall the axe boast itself against him who chops with it? Or shall the saw exalt itself against him who saws*

> *with it? As if a rod could wield itself against those who lift it up, or as if a staff could lift up, as if it were not wood!*
>
> Isaiah 10:15

Inanimate objects cannot take authority over man. Have you ever seen a baseball bat wielding an athlete? Even so, why would we want to position ourselves over God through disobedience? This absurdity is most humbling to the pride of men, who say, "I am my own to do as I please with my life." Quite to the contrary, only God and God alone gives purpose to life. We are used for the high purpose of the Almighty. He is the giver of our lives, talents, and abilities. The proud, wealthy, and mighty among us must still be accountable to God Almighty. In John Donne's Meditation XVII, the poet stresses that no man stands alone self-sufficiently:

> All mankind is of one author [God], and is one volume; when one man dies, one chapter is not torn out of the book, but translated into a better language [higher life]; and every chapter must be so translated...As therefore the bell that rings to a sermon, calls not upon the preacher only, but upon the congregation to come: so this bell calls us all: but how much more me, who am brought so near the door by this sickness....**No man is an island, entire of itself**...any man's death diminishes me, because I am involved in mankind; and therefore never send to know for whom the bell tolls; it tolls for thee (emphasis mine).[20]

An English professor made the following comments on Donne's Meditation:

> The idea that people are not **isolated** from one another, but that mankind is interconnected; and the

vivid awareness of **mortality** that seems a natural outgrowth of a time when death was the constant companion of life. Donne brings these two themes together to affirm that any one man's death diminishes all of mankind, since all mankind is connected; yet that death itself is not so much to be feared as it at first seems (emphasis mine).[21]

The truth is that man can never be but the instrument of God, used by Him for the accomplishment of His divine purposes. No other creation has such purpose for its being, like man does. God uses the elements, seasons, and time to direct man's destiny. Insects that hum in the summer evening do so by the will of God. Flowers opening their tinted blossoms do so by obeying the voice of God. Birds fanning their wings through the air are subjects of the Lord's bidding. God ranked mankind at the height of creation. Our higher level of intelligence substantiates a higher purpose.

Man may be the crown of creation, but he is only a creature set to do God's most delicate and particular work. A basic understanding of history reveals that great nations accomplished specific assignments for God. History records that they did so either willingly or with insubordination. Egypt was directed to free God's chosen people, Israel. Moses was brought up in the Egyptian culture and educational system. God used Moses to lead Israel to freedom. Assyria served as the rod of correction for God. Assyria won many battles, keeping others in fear by their show of force. Babylon held Jerusalem in captivity. Rome proved that restraint or force of law could never replace the liberty of righteousness. Paul's early desire to exterminate Christianity through public persecution was removed during his miraculous encounter with Jesus on the road to Damascus. France showed how the passion for glory led men astray. Even today, France's indecisiveness still influences international world affairs.

England showed what could be accomplished under the inspiration of duty. Sir Winston Churchill led his country to victory by doing what was right for its future survival. Duty requires us to stand up, endure hardship, and fight for what is right for self and others. America, this beautiful land of ours, exemplifies and illustrates the principle of self-government. Our country has fought and continues to fight valiantly to advance freedom around the world. We have illustrated the vast advantages of living in a free society.

Yes, every man and nation is an instrument in the hands of God. In Exodus 9:16, God said to Pharaoh, *"But indeed for this purpose have I raised you up, that I may show My power in you, and that My name may be declared in all the earth."* Charles Wesley, a hymn writer, composed many beautiful hymns that have blessed the nations and won many souls to the Lord. *"Therefore if anyone cleanses himself from the latter, he will be a vessel for honor, sanctified and useful for the Master, prepared for every good work" (2 Timothy 2:21).* Render yourself an instrument unto God.

Chapter 11

We Belong to Jesus
Open Your Heart

"*H*ow often I wanted to gather your children together, as a hen gathers her brood under her wings, but you were not willing" (Luke 13:34)! Like any good parent, God is very mindful to watch over and provide for us. Even when we feel that He is not there, God is there! "*I will not leave you orphans; I will come to you*" *(John 14:18)*. Just as we would not abandon our natural children, God refuses to leave us without His protection. He is so into us that we have whatever we desire from a pure heart. This kindness is one reason He deserves our complete surrender to His will. We must maintain a heart that is sensitive and tenderly open to His leadership.

His supreme desire is to see His children reproduce after the order of His kingdom principles. In John 15:16 we find a clear and direct truth from the Lord. "*You did not choose Me, but I chose you and appointed you that you should go and bear fruit, and that your fruit should remain, that whatever you ask the Father in My name He may give you.*"

A good businessperson is always interested in making a business transaction that shows the promise of a return yield. The business world did not institute this concept. God intended and still intends to enjoy a consistent harvest from His children as we take dominion over the earth and occupy it until the second coming of Jesus. We obtained free volition from the Father to function as we please, with a clear caveat. The caveat is that we exercise our free choice to collaborate with the will of God. As someone once famously said, "Freedom is not the right to do as you please; it is the liberty to do as you ought."

> *For in the day of trouble He [God] will keep me safe in His dwelling; He will hide me in the shelter of His tabernacle and set me high upon a rock.*
> *Psalm 27:5 [NIV]*

In other words, if I open my heart to God's will for my life, then God will personally see that whatever happens to me works for my good under His expressed protection.

Nothing pleases a parent more than to see and enjoy the love, admiration, honor, and respect their children give to them. Each child will express these elements in many different ways, enhancing the overall experience of the parent. God wants to enjoy these experiences with each of His countless children. This expression of love is what I meant by collaborating our free choice with the will of God. By finding God's will and positioning ourselves in the middle, we are free to participate in kingdom rule over the earth, bringing great pleasure to the Father.

Stay Close Enough to Hear

Distressing challenges tend to create barriers in our communication to God. Life events can blockade our ability to communicate with Him, because we fail to yield our will to His. When we hear and follow distinct instructions from

God, our lives elevate to another level. For example, my wife and I took countless hours to train our children to obey our instructions. We are doing pretty well, but we have yet to arrive at perfection. Anyway, my six-year-old son was coming from a soccer game on the other side of a street which he needed to cross in order to get into the family car. His objective was not to consider traffic, but to get to me and into the car. I saw a car quickly approaching the crosswalk and motioned to my son to stop and stand still. He did, and after the car passed, he safely crossed the street. Had he not listened and followed my instructions, his disobedience could have been fatal.

Likewise, we must obey God. We need only do what He tells us, because He knows the beginning and the end. Abraham understood the principle of staying close to God and doing what He said. He had demanded the same of his servants. When *"Abraham was old, well advanced in age" (Genesis 24:1),* he commanded the oldest servant of his house to find a wife for Isaac. Had the servant not been conditioned over the years to obey his master, Abraham, he would have not been chosen for the delicate task. The obedient servant of Abraham sought the favor and kindness of God to help him succeed in his monumental assignment. Subsequently, Isaac married Rebekah (Genesis 24)! Life is full of opportunities that we have to manage while maintaining our closeness to God.

Challenges either bring us closer to God or drive us away from Him. When we push Him away, we deplete His pleasure in us. God expects us to adopt His character and maintain it as a part of our transformation. Anytime we choose not to press toward transforming into the character of God, He is displeased, especially because He always stands ready to help us although we still reject Him by focusing on trivial things.

> *"Come now, and let us reason together," says the Lord, "Though your sins are like scarlet, they shall be as white as snow; though they are red like crimson, they shall be as wool. If you are willing and obedient, you shall eat the good of the land; but if you refuse and rebel, you shall be devoured by the sword."*
> Isaiah 1:18 –20

This flow of Scripture is very powerful. Here we see the Creator making an astonishing appeal to His creation. Normally, this process is quite the reverse. This indication of God's insight and knowledge of future events is both a passion cry unto salvation and a warning for recompense.

God pleads with man from a near standpoint of submission, revealing His humanity while never vacating His dominion as God. *"Come now, and let us reason together"* (v. 18). Hear His heart cry. He wants us to choose a better way than suffering for wrongful choices. He is willing to explore the possibilities if you are. In other words, we have earned the right to be punished severely for wrong choices; however, God generously gives us this opportunity to make our lives right with Him. Please consider His concern for us.

We know that our many transgressions and iniquities towards God require the shedding of blood. Nonetheless, He chose to forgive us, wash us clean, and make us complete again before Him, and He put His Son in our place as ransom. This sacrifice and this sacrifice alone will remove the limitation from our relationship and return us to oneness. God really wants to be with us again and provide our future needs. First, we must make restitution for our wrong. His question is, "Does My overgenerous offer move you any closer to reconciliation? If this offer works for you, then it works for Me." Put away your insolence. Return to Him, for He has our best interests in His heart. The redemption and full restoration of man is the utopia of God's justice in man's favor. Here we see God's unconditional and undying love in action unto the salvation of His people. We serve a great God! Amen.

Chapter 12

My Everything, Oh Most High
Lift Him Up

God said to Moses, *"I AM WHO I AM" (Exodus 3:14)*. This independent, self-sufficient proclamation distinctly captures all that He is and all that is from Him. The Almighty is the only One to declare complete sovereignty above all else with the authority to back His claims!

In my pursuit of God, I purpose to give up everything that creates a distraction from my focus. I have found this renunciation to be the only way to begin knowing the Lord and to experience the mighty power that brought Him back to life again. I believe that God reserves urgent responsibilities for those who dare to yearn for His higher calling. Paul understood this level of desire when he said, *"That I may know Him and the power of His resurrection, and the fellowship of His sufferings" (Philippians 3:10)*. I sense that, until Paul experienced this desire, he could not unlock the door to transformation.

Paul had a burning desire to experience God without limits. He wanted to know more than ever about Jesus. Prior to conversion, Paul opposed the gospel; afterwards, God revealed the kingdom to him. Paul desperately wanted all of

God to unfold in His life. This desire fueled his longing to know Jesus on earth and to spend eternity with Him.

Paul must have said to himself, "To know Jesus I must denounce confidence in all things from the flesh." Paul had received the best of Hebrew education and training. A religious fanatic, he belonged to the strictest sect and lived a blameless life within the law. In outward confidence, he was the best. He had all the privileges that Judaism issued at the time. He relinquished all his privileges, summing them up, putting them aside, and counting them as dirt in comparison with his one gracious hope. Knowing Jesus in his heart and lifting Him up for all to see thrust him forward.

Like Paul, we need to know the power of Jesus' resurrection, which is unlike any other spiritual power, having the ability to lift and restore anew. Acts 9:1-6 records Paul encountering Jesus' resurrection power while traveling the road to Damascus. We also need to understand Paul's sufferings: denying self, repentance, the sting of a convicting conscience, grief for others, the woes of sin, and the overall oppression and afflictions that he had inflicted upon the church. This string of events in the life of Paul prior to his transformation illustrates how the miraculous grace and love of God works in a man to bring about a marvelous restoration. As I read Paul's writings from the time of his reformation, in spite of the many obstacles he endured for the gospel's sake, Paul continually exclaimed that Jesus, who was sent by the Most High God, was his EVERYTHING!

Regardless of our past experiences, a life completely surrendered and fully committed to Jesus can become a dynamic catalyst to witness the gospel. Once you have the experience of Jesus' resurrection power, then you can lift up the name of Jesus with confidence in your heart, make Him Lord, and serve Him as the Savior of the world and its soon-coming King.

Mary and Martha thought they understood this concept until their brother Lazarus lay dead and buried for three days. Jesus delayed His coming to the gravesite for the glory of God. Mary and Martha knew that Jesus was the Son of God. However, they had never seen or heard of mankind being raised from the grave. To believe that their brother could be raised from the dead after four days really was a reach to a distance far from their shore of faith. Jesus arrived at the tomb and consoled the two sisters. Then He discerned that they did not believe God for a present and immediate resurrection for their brother. However, Jesus knew the power of a spoken word. While the sisters grieved over Lazarus, they more than likely said things they never intended, speaking out of their sorrows without faith, like most of us who have grieved. The thought of the death was emotionally too much to bear. Jesus, knowing this grief, provided ample opportunity for them to reverse their speech with faith words. Martha went to meet Him and said, *"Lord if You had been here, my brother would not have died" (John 11:21).* She referred to the physical presence of Jesus. Normally, a person who is ill and near death receives added strength from someone he loves dearly. I believe that the sick person draws enough strength to focus on life and evade death for a season. I believe Martha's point was that Lazarus and Jesus were such good friends that Lazarus would have held on once he saw Jesus' face. Or perhaps she said what she did because she had witnessed Jesus only performing healing miracles, and she had not seen Jesus raise anyone from the dead. Her brother Lazarus was among the first persons Jesus ever raised from the dead. To paraphrase Martha, she said to Jesus, "You were not here. My brother expected to see You. You did not come, and now he is dead." Because Jesus was not there when Lazarus more than likely expected to see Him, especially as he sent for his good friend Jesus, Lazarus resigned to death. Martha cried while talking with

Jesus. Her miracle (Jesus) was talking directly to her, and she did not realize it! The Lord was trying to tell her that He was the Messiah and that the miracle was happening now if she could only believe it! Jesus was waiting for Martha to lift Him up as the right now, resurrecting Messiah! *"And I, if I am lifted up from the earth, will draw all peoples to Myself" (John 12:32).* Wherever Jesus is, He represents the kingdom of God and all of its resources. Martha and Mary agreeing that Jesus could work such a miracle created an atmosphere for the miracle. Jesus will do the miracles that you believe He can do in your life. Lazarus had to rise upon Jesus' command because He was right there representing the kingdom of God. Martha next makes a huge faith statement, *"But even now I know that whatever You ask of God, God will give You" (John 11:22).* Wow! One verse later, in the same breath, Martha activates the spiritual realm with faith words. Jesus now has agreement from Martha because she said, "Whatever Jesus asked of God." My question to you is the same one that Jesus asked, "Do you (Martha) believe that God can raise him (Lazarus)?" Do you really believe that God can actually raise your circumstances to life from the dead? Often we believe that only a specific person can ask God for a precise request. Not so! Your faith has the same potential as my faith, and it will do the same as Jesus' faith, if you believe it and speak it!

When Jesus identified His superiority in verses 25 – 27, Martha replied, *"Yes, Lord, I believe that You are the Christ, the Son of God, who is to **come** into the world" (John 11:27, emphasis mine).* If you find yourself in a support or comfort role to the afflicted, only allow the release of faith words into that atmosphere. Grief begets sorrows. Faith begets wonder-working miracles! Lift Him up, and see His salvation. Oh, Most High!

Glory and Honor

Everything originates with God. Revelation 4:11 states, *"You are worthy, O Lord, to receive glory and honor and power; for You created all things, and by Your will they exist and were created."* This cry was the worship of the twenty-four elders who sat before God in His throne room of heaven. The elders existed for the sole purpose of worshiping God for who He is. Imagine spending your life worshiping the Almighty throughout eternity. I'll remind you that they are merely holding our place until Jesus returns to get us. We will then spend eternity worshiping our Lord as He truly is: high and lifted up on His throne.

God commands and expects continuous worship. Revelation 4:8 says, *"They do not rest day or night saying: Holy, holy, holy, Lord God Almighty, who was and is and is to come!"* Around the throne of God, in John's vision of heaven, were four living creatures bearing a resemblance to a lion, a calf, a man, and a flying eagle. I believe that every time the four creatures glimpsed a deeper revelation of God's glorious being, this worship was their exclamation. Here on earth we use terms like "Wow" or "awesome." Our feeble words, sincere as they might be to honor the presence of God, would do well to follow the exclamation of the four creatures. Apparently, every time they worshiped God, He revealed more of Himself!

Do you ever wonder what would happen if you opened your heart and genuinely honored the high glory of God? Just give God glory for who He is. Do not focus on seeing more of Him. Just praise Him for the level of exposure we already have. I believe that if we operate like heaven, just by reveling in what He has already given us, then God will receive our praise and reveal more of His divine majesty to the manifested purpose of winning souls. If you want more of God, then thank Him for everything He has done in your life to date. He will do more for you as you express your gratefulness for what He has done. Just as you appreciate when others recognize your assistance, God expects and looks for us to honor Him even more for His great acts of compassion in our lives. How can we not give glory to the Lord? We have done nothing ourselves without Him. Yet, He has done everything without us.

For by Him all things were created that are in heaven and that are on earth, visible and invisible, whether thrones or dominions or principalities or powers. All things were created through Him and for Him.
Colossians 1:16

I do not know about you, but when I read this Scripture, I understand clearly who should praise whom! Without God, we would not exist. God is, and because He is, we are. I will say this: had He not decided to see us in His infinite and meticulous mind, our lives would be nonexistent. I thank God for His thoughts towards my life, my purpose, and me. You should do the same!

The Big Harvest

Water from a house hose has very little effect on a farmer's harvest. Conversely, a heavy downpour from the heavens soaks and saturates the ground, creating maximum enrichment to yield a harvest. If you want a small harvest, draw from a small source. If you want a bigger-than-life harvest, draw from the Almighty.

Mount Mitchell in North Carolina has an elevation of 6,684 feet, making it the highest peak of the Appalachian Mountains and eastern North America. While standing on nearby mountain peaks, you would have to look up to Mount Mitchell. Mount Whitney in California measures at 14,505 feet, twice the elevation of Mount Mitchell. However, Mount Everest in Asia stands 29,035 feet in elevation, twice the size of Mount Whitney. Lining the three side by side, a man standing on Mitchell would have to look up to Whitney. Likewise, a man standing atop Whitney would have to look up to Everest.

The same is true of man. Some men have accomplished great things. Be careful not to compare yourself to others. If you stand beside the best, tallest, and greatest of men, they all would have to look up to Christ Jesus. He is always highest above all others. His kingdom has no end, nor does His glory have limiting bounds (Isaiah 9:7).

From Heaven to Earth

Jesus was all of God that He might help us, and all of man that He might sympathize with us. If we say that He was only man, then we are without explanation as to the purpose of His life, His death, His burial, His resurrection, and His ascension. Call the roll of great men present and past; the list is as long as it is distinguished. Nevertheless, none can compare with Jesus because of weaknesses and a sin-flawed nature. Jesus was without sin. *"For He made Him who knew no sin to be sin for us, that we might become the righteousness of God in Him" (2 Corinthians 5:21).*

If you follow the course of a river, you will find at first a muddy stream in the valley. Then, as you go up into the mountain, which is the source of the river, you will find water that is pure and clear. A close study of the life of man reveals muddy streams disguised as sin. Sin forever seeks the low and unguarded areas of our life. Romans 5:20 states, *"But where sin abounded, grace abounded much more."* If a man acquires a truly repentant heart, you will observe his elevation from sin and pollution right into the presence of Jesus. Jesus resides in the high places only.

After coming down from the Mount of Transfiguration, a certain man ran to Jesus and kneeled, crying out, *"My son is an epileptic, have mercy on him" (Matthew 17:15)*. Jesus healed him! On His way to Nain, Jesus met a funeral procession. A poor widow had lost her sole support. Jesus, moved with compassion, brought the young man back to life (Luke 7:11-15)! He also raised Lazarus (John 11:43-44) and the daughter of Jairus (Mark 5:22-24, 35-42) from the dead. Dynamic in personality, Jesus attracted men from all occupations to Him. Matthew left his tax books to become a cowriter of the holy Book. Imagine, a tax collector wrote the first book in the New Testament! Accountants have reason to hope. Christ took a profane fisherman like Simon and turned him into Peter, a great preacher at Pentecost. He took a murderous Pharisee like Saul and changed him into Paul, the mighty apostle to the Gentiles. Then He looked down one day into a little wooded area in South Carolina and saw me, a sinner without the grace of God in my life, picked me up, and changed my course of action. Now I can say:

> I once was an outcast, a stranger on earth,
> A sinner by choice, and an alien by birth;
> I have been adopted, my name written down,
> An heir to a mansion, a robe, and a crown.
> I am a child of the King.
>
> Daniel S. Warner [22]

Jesus surrendered His place in glory temporarily to ensure our complete restoration to God. Better yet, as God the Son, the second entity of the triune Godhead, God sacrificed one-third of His existence to hide our sinful past in His righteousness. Jesus' earthly life serves as an example for all to follow as we look to please God the Father. No other religion or belief system in the history of humanity compares with Christianity, much less records infallible proof about Jesus like it does. Jesus is Lord!

A Present Help

"And it shall come to pass that whoever calls on the name of the Lord shall be saved" (Acts 2:21). Meteorologists can accurately predict when storms are likely to occur and their impact during certain seasons of the year. However, we have no set season in life for such predictions. Life's storms happen when they do, often unexpectedly. You cannot do anything that will exempt you from these storms other than fortify your garrison to deal with them. A storm to one person is completely different from a storm for another. The actual occurrence of the storm should not be your focus until later; rather, focus on how you defend against and get through it.

I like to compare life to a ship at sea. We are all voyaging our way through the sea of life. While our vessels are differently equipped, we are in the same flow of water. The equipment aboard our vessels will determine the success of our travels. Some have taken care to load properly for the journey, while others have left provision to chance. The most important asset on any such vessel is the captain. I recommend Jesus. He has successfully chartered the waters of our journey, and He knows how to bypass every snare and pitfall.

Hezekiah encountered a storm of sickness in his life, bringing him near death's door in 2 Kings 20. Isaiah the prophet, upon direction from God, told Hezekiah to prepare to die (v. 1).

I pause to interject a thought. Someone telling you something does not set that future in stone. You have to know the Word and ways of God to be able to petition Him properly. While I believe that God is subject to His own words, He reserves the express right to change His mind without penalty. *"I will have mercy on whomever I will have mercy, and I will have compassion on whomever I will have compassion" (Romans 9:15).* If you equip yourself with His Word and cry out for mercy, you may find a window of recovery down the road for you, even after the verdict in your storm is cast.

Well, upon receiving the verdict, Hezekiah called out for the mercy of God to reverse His decision (v. 2). Our hearts become amazingly tender when storms arise. Out of the tenderness of Hezekiah's heart came a burning request of God. He recalled his obedient walk before God. *"Remember now, O Lord, I pray, how I have walked before You in truth and with a loyal heart, and have done what was good in your sight" (v. 3).* God remembered the way Hezekiah served Him and heard his bitter cry. As children of God, if we are living an acceptable and pleasing life to God, we have the right through Jesus to petition Him with boldness, fully assured of our request.

Obviously, God moved with compassion and applied mercy to Hezekiah's plight. Before Isaiah got halfway through Hezekiah's courts, he turned around and told Hezekiah the news that his prayer had been answered! God promised to heal the king in a few days. Hezekiah's deepest request also convinced God to stage the winning defense for the city. I was not there when this miracle took place, but I believe Hezekiah felt weightless on his feet every time he thought about what God did for him. *"For by You I can run against a troop; by my God I can leap over a wall" (2 Samuel 22:30).* He will come to your rescue when you call! Oh, Most High!

Chapter 13

His Sacrifice for Us
The Love of God

∞§∞

He bore our agony. Jesus gave His all so that we could be covered in the righteousness of God. The Bible records His punishment as being beyond extreme. *"His visage was marred more than any man, and His form more than the sons of men" (Isaiah 52:14).* Our Lord absorbed the complete retribution of our sins in His physical body. I cannot begin to imagine the pain of His punishment just for me. Even now, my heart pounds unmercifully to know that He endured merciless maltreatment in my place for acts of which He was not guilty, nor would He ever think to commit. Another translation of this same account says, *"At first everyone was appalled. He didn't even look human – a ruined face, disfigured past recognition" (Isaiah 52:14, Message Bible).* You have seen prize fighters compete in the boxing ring for twelve full rounds, inflicting ruthless punches and disfiguring the physical appearance of each other. According to those who personally witnessed Jesus' suffering, the worst of the worst of these paled in comparison to the appearance of Jesus after taking our sin punishment. May we always be reminded of what He did for us through His suffering!

"For God so loved the world that He gave His only begotten Son, that whoever believes in Him should not perish but have everlasting life" (John 3:16). I have friends that really mean a lot to me, and I care for them immensely. I am willing to stand with them and pray God's best for them as a committed friend. On the other hand, I have a few friends for whom I really would die if the occasion warranted. I would actually give my life for this lot. Knowing what I know about them invokes this type of a commitment.

Now let us look at the sacrifice of our Lord once again. The level of commitment He displayed towards us is practically obscure in today's world. God exposes man to an extreme level of unconditional love.

For scarcely for a righteous man will one die; yet perhaps for a good man someone would even dare to die. But God demonstrates His own love toward us, in that while we were still sinners, Christ died for us.

Romans 5:7-8

When you fall in love, things change. You become a different person. The things you used to do no longer have the old effect on you, because you have discovered love. Things people said that used to bother you are like water off of a duck's back. Those things have no impact on your new focus. The thoughts you have are all new, complete, happy thoughts that replace the old ones. You get new friends and go to new places because love is directing and drawing you. When you fall in love with Jesus for all that He gave for you, your life will change, and you will begin to live by new governance with a new focus to have influence. The Lord fell deeply in love with you and proved it with His life by making right every wrong you did. Will you live for Him through your life, telling others of His unconditional and sacrificial love for them?

Think with me for a moment. As a parent, if your child did something wrong but lacked the resources to make his offense right with another, you would have to bridge the gap in his stead to bring restoration, regardless of the price, embarrassment, or sacrifice required. You owe that effort to the person who was wronged, and - yes - your child needs to make his error right. As parents, we probably sacrifice more often than not. However, God made the ultimate one-time sacrifice, which covers all sins and affords complete restoration to all humanity. The person who is offended and the person who brings restoration are one and the same. Man wronged God by introducing sin into the Garden of Eden. God took extraordinary initiative to right the wrong we did to Him. This level of love is extremely rare, if found at all today outside of Christ. Here Almighty God settles the weight of wrong done to Him by His own onto His own shoulders. Even deeper, He asks His only begotten Son to carry the burden of shame, sin, and physical death to balance the entire scenario of sin and its introduction into the Garden. Jesus faced separation from God on the cross to account for our sins. He endured the darkest and loneliest time of His life. On the other side of His obedience to God's will hangs the balance of salvation for humanity.

Because of this level of commitment extended to us by the Father, we can be bold and clear in our recognition and acknowledgement of Jesus as Savior and Lord of all. This extreme sacrifice causes us to hold tight to Him as Redeemer. How else can we express our unending gratitude other than to worship Him as the King of kings and the Lord of lords? Should you find yourself in a place where someone has done everything that the Lord has done for you, then, and only then, should you rethink your gratefulness to our Lord. Let me say that you can search high and low, but no matter where you go, you will not find anybody like Him! Just settle that fact in your heart.

God's love for us through the death of Jesus compels us to show how much we love, value, and honor His sacrifice. We can do so by one way only: that is, to live the entirety of our lives as a thank-you to the One who gave all for us, maximizing the use of every gift He has placed within us. God's love for us has no boundaries. Therefore, He sees us both as we are and as He designed us to be.

A number of us have sacrificed to perform as God purposed for our lives. Nevertheless, a considerable portion of the body of Christ has not purposed to know their destiny or God-given assignment. Our routine, daily cares have desensitized us to a certain degree, temporarily nullifying the love of God. Just like the proverbial frog in a pot of water, we find life to be comfortable, but before long, as the temperature slowly rises, we realize too late a gradual change that compromises the length of our lives. We are to live our lives with the passion of God, bringing the joy of life to each environment that we enter. We are the ambassadorial love answer to the world. The world should not influence us; rather, we should influence it.

Have you ever put off today for tomorrow? Those days become years, and I dare say for some, turn into a lifetime of procrastination, which ends in desolation and the absence of fulfilling their God-given assignments. We are all guilty to a degree. Once you acknowledge the love of God in your life, your life will be changed forever - radically! When I look back over my life and begin to see how God altered the law of time and space to position me right where He wanted me to be for my next season, even when I was being unwise, I'm amazed at His love and forgiveness for me. Even as I write, I recall times when, in the face of challenges from the enemy, He opened doors of escape as I faintly stood on His promises, and when He provided opportunities for advancement in environments where surely I was outnumbered and outwitted. As I spoke, believed, and walked as holy as I could before Him, He just moved on my behalf, simply because He loves me. When I think about all that He has done for me, I realize that His grace is not only sufficient but more than enough to sustain me. I came to realize that not through my influence, authority, or position nor my ability, skill, or aptitude, but only through the relentless love of God were these things added in my life. He loves me, and do you know what? He loves you, too!

God knows that we face temptations constantly. Therefore, He applies His loving grace to elevate us from our constant challenges. He may not take away your challenge because He is using it to build your character. However, He will supply perfect love and sufficient grace for you to engage your challenge and defeat it with the abilities He has given you. You can make it!

His Love

One definition of love is justice: love in action. The action of love produces life. God always demonstrates perfect love through action. Jesus' crucifixion, death, and resurrection are all examples of love in action. John 3:16 states, *"For God so loved the world he [gave] His only begotten Son, that whoever believes in Him should not perish but have everlasting life."* Love gives! If you love someone, you will give something to sustain his or her life. God allowed Jesus to suffer a lonely death while giving His life for us. He gave through action. Acts 3:6 records Peter saying, *"Silver and gold I do not have, but what I do have I give you: In the name of Jesus Christ of Nazareth, rise up and walk."* As Peter and John entered the temple, a lame man was asking charity of all who passed by. Peter had nothing but love to give. When he gave love in the name of our Lord, the lame man walked. Love is an action that produces life.

Subsequently, God's love represents diversity and inclusion. In Acts 10:34-35, Peter says, *"In truth I perceive that God shows no partiality. But in every nation whoever fears Him and works righteousness is accepted by Him."* Those who claim to be unloved by Him have not allowed themselves to be touched within the core of their hearts. Once they let Him in, they will experience a love divine as never before. Jesus understood the importance of what He did on the cross. He, through the agent of the Holy Spirit, helps us to endure that which He has already conquered.

We prove our clear and visible love of Jesus by keeping His statutes. John 15:10 says, *"If you keep my commandments, you will abide in my love, just as I have kept my Father's commandments and abide in His love."* No matter what you are facing in your life, focus on the love of Jesus, who is the lover of your soul. His love surpasses our highest knowing, beyond our understanding. This kind of love is without explanation. The foundation of it is trust.

We must trust that God loves us and that His love will sustain us. Trusting His love means staying inside His will. Your protection is guaranteed within God's covering. Following His instructions helps you to enjoy His love more than any amount of sacrifice you could ever offer to earn His love. You cannot earn God's love. The only thing you can do is to receive it and give it back to Him and others in forms that are acceptable to each. Receive the love!

After receiving the Master's love, give it away quickly, and get some more to give away! *"He who did not spare His own Son, but delivered Him up for us all, how shall He not with Him also freely give us all things?" (Romans 8:32).* If God can freely give us Jesus as a love sacrifice, we can surely give to others freely the love we receive from Him. Love is something that you enjoy by not keeping. The more you give away, the more you receive. Your love-giving tank should always be full. You have to have love in order to give it away. Give it away!

Love One Another

"A new commandment I give you that you love one another" (John 15:12). Listen, the test of a man's power is no longer dependent upon a show of arms, athleticism, financial wealth, or intelligence. The real test of power within a man is the simple, fundamental virtue of love. Did you feed the hungry? Did you visit those in need of comfort? Did you perform those little, nameless, unnoticeable acts of kindness, which are the better portion of a good man's life? Are they visible, those fruits of the Spirit, which grow largely from love: long suffering, gentleness, sympathy, understanding, generosity, and charity? Are you getting along any better with your neighbors? Do you even know your neighbors?

As we are just visiting, have you mustered the strength and courage needed to break down the artificial barriers between you and others? How about loving those in different circumstances from yours? Have you gotten to the level of forgiving and forgetting unsolicited insults, misuse, slander, and those taking advantage of you? You see, being churchy and quoting a few Scriptures from rote memory is not necessarily a bad thing. However, those actions deplete your effectiveness as a Christian if they have no power. Don't tell me so much. I would rather see your life, which is more easily identifiable.

Moreover, if you are afraid to love, you are afraid to live. Love is an indispensable element in human life. A woman once wrote explaining her suicide: "I am killing myself because I have never sincerely loved any human being in all my life." This statement is very troubling, because lack of the very thing that both created and sustained her life took it away. Imagine losing the capacity to love! Listen to what the Lord is saying. Love one another, because love is both healthy and vital to sustaining human life. This woman was obviously afraid of becoming vulnerable to someone else. So she never got beyond herself long enough to discover or give someone a chance to love her. This story reminds me of Tennyson's "In Memoriam":

> I hold it true, whatever befall,
> I feel it, when I sorrow most;
> 'Tis better to have loved and lost,
> Than never to have loved at all.[23]

Love should be our daily meal, if not an essential supplement. The matter is unmistakable. We must take care to love, or we shall become hopeless, frustrated, and ultimately defeated.

Love Is Inclusive

A woman who was about fifty years old was seated next to a man from a different culture which she did not prefer. Obviously disturbed by this arrangement, she called the flight attendant. "Madam, what is the matter?" the flight attendant asked. "You obviously do not see, then?" she responded. "You placed me next to this repulsive man. I did not agree to sit next to someone from such a repugnant group. Give me an alternative seat." "Be calm, please," the attendant replied. "Almost all the seats on this flight are taken. I will go to see if another seat is available." She went away and came back a few minutes later. "Madam, just as I thought, no other seats are available in economy class. I spoke to the captain, and he informed me that no seats are available in the business class, either. All the same, we still have one seat in first class." Before the woman could reply, the attendant continued: "It is unusual for our company to permit someone from economy class to sit in first class. However, given the circumstances, the captain feels that making someone sit next to someone so disgusting would be scandalous." The attendant turned to the man and said, "Sir, if you would like, please collect your hand luggage; a seat awaits you in first class." At that moment, the other passengers, who were shocked by what they had just witnessed, stood up and applauded.[24]

> He drew a circle that shut me out,
> Heretic, rebel, thing to flout,
> But love and I had the wit to win,
> He drew a circle that took me in.
>
> Edwin Markham[25]

True love will embrace the rejected, include others regardless of their circumstances, and end envious and petty backbiting. For you see, Jesus accepted you, all humanity, and me when we did not deserve to be accepted. Included in His acceptance were the mean, divisive, and rebellious among us. I did not learn that truth from a book but from my mother. With tears caressing her furrowed cheeks, she sang:

> Jesus included me, yes, He included me,
> When the Lord said, "Whosoever," He included me;
> Jesus included me, yes, He included me,
> When the Lord said, "Whosoever," He included me
>
> Johnson Oatman, Jr.[26]

God continually loves us with patience that asks for no explanation. He allowed us to deny Him, mock Him, betray Him, and crucify Him that we may learn to love Him. In the eyes of God, love is sharing. In 1875, Karl Marx said, "From each according to his ability, to each according to his need."[27] His statement is a definition of love, like the love

Jesus wants us to show one another. Your consuming interest should not be in income but rather output. Life is not about how much or what you get; it is all about how much or the quality of what you give to others. Anything shy of the focus on giving is manipulation. If you follow God's design for love, you will always get what you need when you need it!

Teenagers are buried under tremendous pressures generated by current trends, styles, and behavioral patterns discovered and promoted as normal for their generation by the world's standard. My teenage daughter has consistently and effectively been able to flow with these while still representing holiness. She has established herself as someone governed by godly standards with great impact on her peers as well as others who know her. She has not surrendered to the empty and chaotic temptations of the world. My daughter has made me very proud of all that she does. Her deep sense of excellence permeates her and drives her to do what is right. While I know that doing right has not always been easy for her, she has earned my highest trust and support for the decisions she has made to stay the course of living godly. Her love for the things of God and right actions has made the difference in her life, especially surviving the challenges and drama of her teenage years to date. I am very proud of her! She is living a committed life.

Love is commitment: *"Having loved His own which were in the world, He loved them to the end" (John 13:1)*. Jesus knew the level of endurance and focus required to conquer the daily circumstances of His time. Words followed action. Today, we spend a considerable amount of time telling others what we intend to do and trying to convince them. People are not too fond of your intent to make something happen. However, after you have finished, you can take all the time you need to explain your accomplishment. Evidently, the entire world has now adopted the motto of the state of Missouri: "show me." Jesus did more doing than telling.

His short but very influential few years of visible ministry centered on miracles that revealed the love commitment of the Father towards us. God loves us so much that He sent the perfection of heaven to earth to bring restoration.

My wife has no doubt about my commitment and love for her and our family. We established this clear understanding between us over many years of marriage. My words have meaning to my wife because my committed actions over time brought the credibility needed to reinforce them. So when I tell her that I love her, she immediately calls to mind the many ways I've showed my commitment to her. Having a stockpile of love-in-action memories to remind her of my commitment makes accepting my words as truth easy for her. This trust brings a great comfort in our marriage.

Love is service. A man hurried into a church asking if the service was over. The immediate reply stunned him, "The worship is over, but the service is just beginning." You see, service is not about you receiving something. Service is what you give to another. From God's view, Jesus served humanity through the gift of His own life. Serving your way to greatness takes on a completely new meaning when you understand God's way of order. If you love someone, serve him or her.

My father was the ultimate server. He had the ability to see a need before it happened. I clearly remember him giving my three brothers and me advice about the many opportunities we would face as grown men if we did not develop good character. He was so convinced that character was important that he disciplined himself to illustrate what good character looked like for his four sons and four daughters. His indelible acts of service are the foundation of my character today. He gave us his character through daily interactions and firm guidance, helping to mold us into men and women who willingly serve others. For example, my father would not uncommonly spend a considerable amount of time with anyone needing encouragement. He had a unique ability to walk into a room, pick out the person with the most challenges in life, and speak words of encouragement to reengage him. Subsequently, others could see how passionate he was about life and the welfare of others less fortunate. He saturated us with the concept to build up, promote, and help to advance others. He taught us how to live a lifestyle of giving. When you give to others from a heart of service, you often meet an unspoken need by doing for others what they could not do for themselves!

Love is sacrifice. Do you remember the story of the young man who was condemned to die during the reign of bloody Cromwell in England?[28] His execution had been set for sunset at the toll of the bell from the tower. His sweetheart heard the verdict, and just before the tolling of the curfew, she climbed to the top of the tower and put her tender hands around the clapper of the bell. The sexton, who was deaf, pulled the cord as usual but could not tell that the bell had not sounded. As the bell did not sound, the execution was suspended. Rushing down from the tower, the faithful lover rushed to Cromwell and stood in his presence. Poet Rose Hartwick Thorpe unraveled the scene in this fashion:

> O'er the distant hills comes Cromwell. Bessie sees him; and her brow,
> Lately white with sickening horror, has no anxious traces now.
> At his feet she tells her story, shows her hands, all bruised and torn;
> And her sweet young face, still haggard, with the anguish it had worn,
> Touched his heart with sudden pity, lit his eyes with misty light.
> "Go! your lover lives," said Cromwell. "Curfew shall not ring to-night!"[29]

Love is a sacrifice. Jesus climbed Calvary and placed His hands around the clapper of the bell, saving us from a guilty verdict. Jesus proved His love for us ultimately by sacrificing His life. When I think about His goodness and what He did for me alone, I am humbled that He would call me friend. I am overwhelmed at the very thought of His kindness towards me, although His level of sacrifice demands an intimate relationship. He affectionately calls me His friend. Glorious is the name of Jesus!

As I consider all the wonders You have made,
The universe within Your hand,
My heart need never be afraid;
By faith I stand.

Your power living in me,
Your powerful ways,
Jesus, Almighty God,
All creation sings Your praise.

Glorious, excellent is Your name in all the earth!
Marvelous, wonderful is Your name in all the earth!
    Frank Montgomery and Bruce Monthy[30]

He Took Our Place

We have an unconscious habit of saying, "he took my place, spot, or turn." We do so out of selfishness. If we really think with the full revelation of what Jesus did on the cross about the meaning of this phrase, we would use it sparingly. The impact from a clear understanding of what Christ accomplished for us on the cross gives the phrase a redemptive influence. When we say the phrase, it should have significance. A fleshly response to a natural activity with little significance undermines the use of this phrase.

Recognizing and accepting a spiritual revelation that created and constructed our eternal existence is the true condition befitting: "*He took my place.*" That someone was Jesus! He took the sting of death for our many sins that we may live our lives unto righteousness, commemorating His remarkable sacrifice by telling others what He did for us.

God gave us a wonderful life to live for His good pleasure. Living our life to its fullest and telling others about His goodness shows God our gratefulness for the precious gift He gave in our place. God's simple request to us is to tell others about His love. We should tell others even if they do not believe. We are to tell them even if they do not receive the truth that Jesus died for them. We are to shout at the top of our voices that His love never ends. His patience eternally waits for them to end their unnecessary suffering through a life of surrendered obedience to Him. God wants them to know that His love is available and free to all who would accept the fact that Jesus took our place of sin punishment! Yes! He took your place!

Chapter 14

All Things Work Together
He Provides from His Abundance

Many days in my early years, I wanted nothing to do with the gospel. I did what was right because my father was a preacher for fifty-eight years; yes, I am a preacher's kid (PK). Of the fifty-eight years, he was a pastor for the last thirty-six of them. However, I did not know that God was working for my good.

When I was growing up in South Carolina and throughout my international travels around the world until the age of twenty-eight, I had no idea that God could miraculously heal my body from sickness. Seeing Him turn things around when all was against me, calm my doubts and fears, or provide abundance in the place of lack, was out of the question. I will tell you that, had I known these things earlier in my life, my early years would have been different, I'm sure. With that caveat, let me say that not all is lost; the start and completion of this book by its author proves that the Scriptures are real. *"Now we know that all things work together for good to those who love God, to those who are the called according to His purpose" (Romans 8:28).*

I am here writing this book because it is a part of my destiny. I did not earn this position through a focused preparation or remarkable literary skills. I had no desire to write a book. Scripture found in 2 Timothy 1:9 states, *"Who has saved us and called us with a holy calling, not according to our works, but according to His own purpose and grace which was given to us in Christ Jesus before time began."* Listen, I would have passed on this opportunity had the decision been up to me. I told you earlier how I missed opportunity in my earlier years. But God! My honor is that He both preserved and positioned me to accomplish this particular work for His glory. This project is a miracle, as my writing skills throughout high school and the first two years of college did not qualify me for the assignment of writing this book. I am so glad that God always equips those He calls to accomplish great things for Him. He will provide everything you need and make all things work for your good.

Healing

Based on the foundation of the cross, for a believer to be sick with no recovery is spiritually illegal. Galatians 3:13 says, *"Christ has redeemed us from the curse of the law, having become a curse for us (for it is written, 'Cursed is everyone who hangs on a tree')."* You must accept and believe what took place on Calvary's cross in order to tap into your healing recovery. Anything short of believing that Jesus hung on the cross for the sins of the entire world would limit the power of God in your life. Not believing that Jesus died at Calvary, taking away our sin, shame, and sickness would mock His sacrifice. Who else would endure the death that Jesus suffered for us? No one but the Lord is your answer.

During my service in the Marine Corps, I developed an aggravating pain in my abdomen for which doctors could not find a solution. Doctors conducted many examinations with different prognoses, but to no avail. One day I got sick and tired of going to medical appointments for unfruitful examinations. I simply asked God to heal my body and restore me. What a difference that prayer made! God healed my body. *"Heal me, O Lord, and I shall be healed; save me, and I shall be saved, for You are my praise" (Jeremiah 17:14).*

While I was teaching at the FAA Academy, my friend Gloria approached me one day with a deep sense of discouragement and sorrow. I asked her what was bothering her. She told me that a recent medical examination revealed that she had a sign of cancer cells in her body. We were standing at a water fountain in a hallway with a heavy traffic flow. I asked if I could pray for her on one condition, and she accepted. My condition was that we would pray right then at the fountain because she informed me there. I refused to hide in a closet and pray. I prayed a simple but sincere prayer for her. A few weeks later, she excitedly called with news that the cells were no longer present! She said, "Can you believe it? The cells are gone!" I said, "Yes! I believed before I first prayed for you." God can use anyone to do anything He desires. Just believe and be willing and available! I was willing; Gloria agreed. And God did the healing! *"For I am the Lord who heals you" (Exodus 15:26).* Amen.

Jesus endured death and the grave, paying our debt in full. His resurrection by the power of the Holy Spirit validates our victory in Him. If you can believe this foundational truth of the gospel, then you have the victory in your healing. He is not dead but alive forevermore!

Hallelujah, Jesus is alive!
Death has lost
Its victory,
And the grave
Has been denied.

Jesus lives forever.
He's alive; He's alive!

He's the Alpha and Omega;
The first and last is He.
The curse of sin is broken,
And we have perfect liberty.
The Lamb of God has risen.
He's alive; He's alive!

Ron Kenoly[31]

If you are experiencing sickness and disease in your physical body, healing is available to you from the Almighty. If you are healthy, then I encourage you to take daily doses of Word vitamins to keep you healthy and strong. Divine health is just as important as divine healing. The first prevents the latter in most cases. Now, make this daily faith confession, and receive restoration in your body. According to Galatians 3:13, "I am redeemed from the curse of the Law through Christ Jesus. Therefore, I no longer have sickness and disease in my body." Look up similar Scriptures to help your healing process while following your doctor's expert care.

Favor

Imagine how Mary must have felt and thought at her unlikely and unexpected greeting from the Lord. Luke 1:28 states, *"Rejoice highly favored one, the Lord is with you; blessed are you among women!"* Wow! What an opportunity to be unique among multitudes! At any given time throughout the world, many women are giving birth. Some have single births of a child with superior abilities. Some have multiple births under extraordinary circumstances. Unique and wonderful as these experiences and those of countless others are, no other woman has had the patent privilege of the Virgin Mary.

The Lord Himself sent word to Mary that He chose her for the responsibility of mothering the Christ, Savior of the world. Just like God favored Mary, He wants to favor you with a special assignment tailored for your abilities. Live for Him, and find the favor He so desperately wants you to have. So I say to you, "Rejoice highly favored one; the Lord is with you! Blessed are you among all!"

Peace

Our fast-paced society offers no time for maintaining inner peace as we strive to meet the demands of our varied schedules. Psalm 119:165 says, *"Great peace have those who love Your law, and nothing causes them to stumble."* The way a person demonstrates self-control during troubled times give insight into his character in times of quietness. A person with bad nerves cannot withstand frustrating conditions. A nervous person should carefully manage himself or avoid crowds and conflicts that might set him off. If he watches an engaging athletic event, he cannot stand to watch much of it. Likewise, a Christian who is weak in battle with the enemy cannot withstand too many attacks. A weak soldier on the battlefield will not get the job done. We must determine and condition ourselves in the Word of God to be valiant warriors, able to withstand the hardship of battle by maintaining a posture of peace.

While doctors prescribe rest for nervous conditions, God gives us the Holy Spirit to strengthen our weakness. In spite of the chaos that life offers, we can have peace by realizing the power of God, who says, *"Be still and know that I am God" (Psalm 46:10).* God spoke this comfort when the disciples were in the middle of a storm and expecting overwhelming circumstances, circumstances possibly leading to destruction. The time was much like now, post-September 11, where a selected few seem to rob the world of a favorable peace. What should we do? I suggest we follow the instructions of signs placed at railroad crossings: stop, look, and listen. Stop for what? Stop trying to please ourselves, and start to please God. Where should we look? Psalm 121:1 states, *"I will lift up my eyes to the hills; from whence comes my help? My help comes from the Lord, who made heaven and earth."* Develop the eyesight of Abraham when God called him out of his tent. When we listen, what do we want to hear? Listen for the clear guidance of the Holy Spirit. John 4:10 says, *"And when he brings out his own sheep, he goes before them; and the sheep follow him, for they know his voice."* We will find His peace for our lives if we are quiet as we listen to follow the instructions of His voice.

> Silence is the element in which great things fashion themselves.
>
> Thomas Carlyle[32]

The thoughts we harbor and the words we speak compromise our state of peace. We know that words create images that stir emotions. That all commercials operate from this premise is a proven fact. To sell a product or provide a service, advertisers choose specific words that create a desirable sight picture. This picture taps into the emotions of viewers, convincing them that they really need what they are experiencing through their senses. When the viewer sees the product while shopping or hears about the service in a commercial, he experiences a direct connection from what he sees on the shelf to his exposure through the commercial. The next obvious step is to take action to purchase the item. Violation of our peace happens the same way. If we allow ourselves exposure to the wrong information, the exposure will paint a canvas of worry and frustration within us. As we focus continually on the worry and frustration, they generate negative emotions to accompany our fears and concerns. After a season of neglecting biblical principles, we buy into the fear and act on it. Once we act on it, we have created a condition reversible only by purging our minds with the Word. This simple process occurs many times within our person, in everything we do. The core of our being centers on our ability to maintain peace.

Paul made this connection in his writing to the Philippians. Philippians 4:7 states, *"And the peace of God, which surpasses all understanding, will guard your hearts and minds through Christ Jesus."* While we have a critical role to play in maintaining inner peace by filtering everything we experience through the purifying Word of God, ultimately only the God kind of peace really makes us work like He designed us to work. This peace frees us from anxiety and unwanted pressures from the world.

Chapter 15

Prosperity
Withdraw from Your Deposits

If you show sound resource management with little, God will increase your capacity for more. I think we make the fatal mistake of treating little like it's nothing in hopes of getting more with which to show our good stewardship. God's way demands faithfulness with little before He increases our responsibility with much. *"Well done, good and faithful servant; you were faithful over a few things, I will make you ruler over many things" (Matthew 25:21).*

For example, Ruth was faithful to Naomi when Naomi had nothing but her heritage through a parcel of land. Eventually, both Ruth and Naomi profited through Boaz from the parcel. Ruth ended up marrying Boaz, a man of great wealth, taking her place in history among the genealogy of Jesus Christ (Matthew 1:5). Ruth prospered in various ways: through marriage, giving birth to a son, and continuing the family bloodline. However, her finances, although great, were among the least of her prosperity. While financial prosperity is a promise from God, you can prosper in many other ways besides your finances: mind, body, and soul! *"Beloved,*

I pray that you may prosper in all things and be in health, just as your soul prospers" (3 John 1:2).

I once had an account for which I owed a payment. The company told me what I owed, and I somehow overpaid the balance, leaving me with a credit. Now hear me carefully. Large companies become financial giants because of unclaimed, overpaid credit. My overpaid credit was two dollars and seventy-nine cents. I called the company to close the account and asked to have my credit paid to me. The account representative was shocked both that I was aware of the credit and that I asked for a remittance. The impression I got was that millions of people overlook the wise stewardship of collecting overpaid credit. This impression overwhelmingly surprised me. When the account representative gathered himself, he asked if I really wanted the two dollars and seventy-nine cents. I told him yes! I asked him what would happen to the money if I declined to collect it. He told me that the company would keep it. Right then, an equation rose up inside me: ten million times two dollars and seventy-nine cents equals twenty-seven million, nine hundred thousand dollars. This amount is a huge, noncompetitive profit for the company. You leave money on the table, and the company profits. Never walk away from resources that belong to you.

Had I simply given it to the company, my gain would be that my account was paid in full, closed, and reported in good standing to the credit bureaus. Likewise, the company enhances its collection portfolio, sells my credit history, and adds my unclaimed overpayment to its profit margins. Instead of leaving the $2.79 on the table, I recovered it and sowed it as seed toward increase. Look, you can either increase the kingdom of God or increase the world's economy. I will say this: you should increase the one that guarantees increase for you. Do you believe that little becomes much with good stewardship, or do you believe that you should relax good stewardship until you amass much? Prosperity starts with wise stewardship of little. How do you view prosperity?

My wife and I tithe faithfully. We give generously on many occasions for the gospel's sake. We have many seeds sown into various good soils. While we have received harvests, we also know that we can make faith withdrawals compounded on the seeds we have sown. When we give, we expect harvests. We are careful to assign a purpose to each seed and water it in faith until it is ready to harvest. God always brings the harvest increase. Amen.

How did Joshua view prosperity from God? He purposed to recall and recognize descriptive details about how God had provided for Israel. *"I have given you a land for which you did not labor, and cities which you did not build, and you dwell in them; you eat of the vineyards and olive groves which you did not plant" (Joshua 24:13).*

God seems to me to be serious about providing all that we need for us. Joshua gathered all the tribes of Israel together along with the elders, judges, and officers. He gave a briefing on the divine intervention of God to the nation. Israel, in their haste for national recognition, had become insensitive to their glorious history. Contacts and association with other nations were leading them to forget their spiritual heritage, and they desired to be like the other nations. Therefore, Joshua remembered their deep devotion to God during their long and difficult journey through the wilderness. He had seen their radiant faith during the dark days of slavery. He shared with them their hopes and aspirations for happier days and a better life under the promises of God. Those good days had come, and Joshua saw their glowing faith shifted. The people's power and prestige grew. They began to forget about God. They wanted fatherly provisions from God without childlike obedience.

They wished to be the chosen people of God, but they wanted the privilege of choosing their own course of action.

As I look at our world today, I marvel at the striking similarities between this ancient account and our present time. Our advancement in various fields has rendered us self-centered, independent, and at times arrogant, neglecting the things of God. We have plenty of distractions available to misdirect our relationships with God if we remain unaware. We are living in a time when a do-it-yourself spirit and technological advances steer our culture. The focus on higher education and rote learning obstructs faith in God for most. The perspective of getting all the education you can without learning about God is greatly misdirected! We must have a balance. If you err on either side, err in favor of God knowledge. Revelation wisdom from God is the beginning of true, life-sustaining knowledge for man. Let's be very careful not to ignore or turn away from God, our Provider. Let's learn from Israel's neglect and Joshua's passion to keep our focus on the true blessings of God.

Make in your life a habit of being generous in all that you do. Be generous with your time to others for a productive end. Be generous with your talents to encourage others with similar interests and not to bury their gifts. Be generous with your finances by seeking ways to bless others. *"But who am I, and who are my people, that we should be able to offer so willingly as this? For all things come from You, and of Your own we have given You" (1 Chronicles 29:14).* Recognize this truth: your prosperity does not belong to you. It comes from God, and He owns all of it. Be generous in your giving!

Instructions on Giving

Be generous! Cultivate and maintain a lifestyle of giving to the things of God and the lives of those less fortunate than you. *"In the morning sow your seed, and in the evening do not withhold your hand; for you do not know which will prosper, either this or that, or whether both alike will be good" (Ecclesiastes 11:6).*

Give for the gospel's sake. Do not be manipulated by words of persuasion or sad, sorry stories designed to influence the amount of your giving. You can find clear guidance for giving in 2 Corinthians 2:9, which says, *"So let each one give as he **purposes in his heart**, not grudgingly or of necessity; for God loves a cheerful giver" (emphasis mine).* You and only you should determine the amount you give to anyone, on any occasion, under any circumstance, unless God prompts you otherwise. As a believer and doer of the Word, this responsibility is yours, like reading your Bible daily, praying, voting, etc. God has given us free will to manage our affairs according to His Word and within its parameters. Do not be manipulated, as this weakness will impact your spiritual harvest, because you have not purposed in your heart to give.

Subsequently, do not become callous and refuse to give because of manipulating circumstances you may have experienced. God gave us Jesus, a very generous gift. Therefore, He expects us to give to the effective works that advance the gospel with a generous and delightful heart, knowing that this type of giving pleases Him.

Prefer others. *"It is more blessed to give than to receive" (Acts 20:35).* A lifestyle of giving, meeting the known and unknown needs of others, brings deep joy to the giver. While we were at our worst, God sacrificed Jesus as a gift to us so that we may inherit the righteousness of God. Elevating, restoring, and advancing others are kingdom practices we should observe to fulfill Scripture.

Instructions on Receiving

Now concerning receiving, receiving as well as giving is the will of God. Giving is just better. God outlined in

Scripture in very descriptive detail how the return on your investing into the kingdom God will come back to you.

Give, and it will be given to you: good measure, pressed down, shaken together, and running over will be put into your bosom. For with the same measure that you use, it will be measured back to you.
Luke 6:38

In fact, you should receive after giving, not immediately, although you may. Usually, you will experience a time of seed germination. Farmers don't plant at night and reap in the morning. When you give your seed offering, expect a specific harvest! If you sow without expecting a harvest, you undermine the divine process of God. *"For God so loved the world that He gave His only begotten Son, that whoever believes in Him should not perish but have everlasting life" (John 3:16).* He sowed Jesus as a precious gift to us. Therefore, He expects a harvest based on the seed He sowed. Isaiah 52:15 states, *"So shall He sprinkle many nations."* God's expected harvest is that all be saved!

What's His is Mine

My six-year-old daughter was in the room one day when my wife and I were discussing the detailed charges on a recent phone bill. My wife and I thought the charges for a particular service were too much. However, my daughter said, "That's not a lot of money." I replied, "Show me the particular amount from your money." She got out of my lap and started walking toward a piggy bank where we put loose change for our kid's savings. I quickly assessed her intentions and said, "That's not your money, because I put it in there; that's my money." She said, "I know it's your money, but you gave it to me. So it's mine." God reminded me to be a generous giver through that simple act of faith that my daughter demonstrated. What He has belongs to us, so long as we have the right intent in our heart to use it. Wow! I realized that the reason the Lord expects us to be generous givers is that He is supplying what we are giving. The more we give, the more He supplies. Don't misunderstand me: please be wise in your giving. Give into good soil for worthy occasions that will promote the gospel. Nonetheless, give out of the generosity of your heart while being obedient to God, and see if He will not increase your supply inventory.

Wisdom and knowledge are granted to you; and I will give you riches and wealth and honor, such as none of the kings have had who were before you, nor shall any after you have the like.
2 Chronicles 1:12

God greatly prospered Solomon because he asked for wisdom and knowledge to lead God's people. Solomon had a consistent history of giving to God. I will make two points from this Scripture.

First, always ask of God something that complements His agenda. Genuinely identify His concerns for His people. Help promote kingdom principles, and God will provide for you in the process. You always want your desires to touch the heart of God and display His love for people.

Second, God wants you to be prosperous. In this scenario, God was the One who initiated the subject of "riches and wealth." Solomon never mentioned prosperity in his request! He specifically asked for wisdom and knowledge to lead God's people. God knew that a person with His wisdom and knowledge could steward limitless wealth. Therefore, the cry of Solomon's heart caused God to increase him like no other. The Bible recorded Solomon having no lack throughout his life. Wow!

Prosperity is one of God's ways to reward us, just like we reward our kids. Prosperity is not a payment, because He does not owe us anything. The debt is ours; we owe Him. Prosperity is not a form of manipulation, because all power belongs to God. Prosperity has to be a gift or reward for our obedience to Him. We do the same with our kids. They always want to know: What's In It For Me (WIIFM)? What do I get? God tunes into this popular radio station, WIIFM, and addresses this question in every conversation He has with us. He answers this question whether we ask it or not. When God addresses our needs, He also looks for ways to prosper us before we tune into the local station: WIIFM. What an awesome God!

Prosperity belongs to you. In 2 Chronicles 32:30 we see that *"Hezekiah prospered in all his works."* Humility goes a long way with God. It will win the favor of God in your life, because you submit to His sovereign will. Let's study Hezekiah a little closer.

> *Hezekiah had very great riches and honor. And he made himself treasuries for silver, for gold, for precious stones, for spices, for shields, and for all kinds of desirable items; storehouses for the harvest of grain, wine, and oil; and stalls for all kinds of livestock, and folds for flocks. Moreover he provided cities for himself, and possessions of flocks and herds in abundance; for God had given him very much property. This same Hezekiah also stopped the water outlet of Upper Gihon, and brought the water by tunnel to the west side of the City of David. Hezekiah prospered in all his works.*
> *2 Chronicles 32:27–30*

As I study and present this information to you, no one should ever convince you to choose poverty over prosperity.

Obviously, God does not have a problem with wealth and riches. The more I understand God, the more I see that seeing us grovel in poverty displeases Him because of all He did to position us for prosperity. Conscientiously choosing poverty over prosperity is a mockery to God. He has given too much for you to choose so little in life. Rise up, and receive what belongs to you. The riches of heaven belong to you as a joint heir to the treasures of heaven with Christ Jesus! Psalm 34:8 states, *"Oh, taste and see that the Lord is good; blessed is the man who trusts in Him!"* You have to purpose to allow yourself to receive the prosperity that God has stored for you.

Trust God's Economy

Living under the provision of God is the best life possible. Man's economy does not influence God's economy. In fact, whenever man's economy is in a financial downfall or just flat lined, God does His best work to show Himself strong. He does not need man for anything! After all, man inscribes "In God we trust" on his currency. You would do better to trust God over the likes of man.

> *And we know that all things work together for good to those who love God, to those who are the called according to His purpose. For whom He foreknew, He predestined to be conformed to the image of His Son.*
>
> *Romans 8:28*

This verse describes God's all-inclusive insurance plan. God guarantees to deliver. Amazing! Other insurance plans provide limited coverage of things like natural disasters, "acts of God", etc. I like God's plan better, because those "acts" that the others do not cover, He covers. As a matter of fact, my premium is paid for life, and I'll never need to increase coverage, because God's plan includes every imaginable eventuality, known and unknown. If you don't have this kind of coverage, change your plan!

Recently, I received a phone call from a national pest-control company representative who serviced our house for spiders. Because of the climate in the Pacific Northwest, we experience lots of spiders. First, he confirmed that we had cancelled our service. Then he asked if we would reconsider continuing our service contract to help balance his company's employment due to the downfall of the economy. I told him that the reason we terminated the contract was that the company had solved our insect problem. We no longer needed the service. He pressed me by asking a second time to reconsider. I told him no.

While I understood his fear of the economy's impact on his company, he failed to recognize my compliment. His company had worked itself out of a job. Accordingly, he would have been wise to stop trying to manipulate customers to gain additional business. We had given his company one full year of business and heard from him very few times. Now that the economy was failing, communication to us was suddenly important.

Learn to live your life beyond focusing on what you can get. *"If in this life only we have hope in Christ, we are of all men the most pitiable" (1 Corinthians 15:19).* God wants you to live a prosperous and happy life that promotes the riches of eternity, not earthly gains. You are designed to manage wealth and lots of it! *"For you know the grace of our Lord Jesus Christ, that though He was rich, yet for your sakes He became poor, that you through His poverty might become rich" (2 Corinthians 8:9).* Listen, Jesus paid the debt of poverty in full for us. Do not accept an impoverished lifestyle. Doing so directly insults our Lord after all He did to secure our prosperity. You have a BIG God. Have

BIG dreams, and live your life with a clear alignment of your sight to see them happen! *"With men this is impossible, but with God all things are possible" (Matthew 19:26).* In the uncertain development of the world's economy, many will worry and become anxious for fear of not having enough resources. I encourage you to trust the economy of God, making Him your source. *"If you can believe, all things are possible to him who believes" (Mark 9:23).*

Chapter 16

Freedom and Restoration
Repent

> *For the law was given through Moses, but grace and truth came through Jesus Christ.*
>
> *John 1:17*

The first word of the gospel is *repent*. Webster's 1828 Dictionary tells us that to repent means to creep.[28] Follow me with this thought. Have you ever seen a puppy wait for its mother's response by slowly creeping towards her with its head low between its paws, eyes begging upward, and tail between the legs as if it were repenting and praying for forgiveness? The puppy creeps forward, ever so slowly, so as to not move ahead of forgiveness. Well, those of us who accept responsibility for our sin actions do likewise with God. Ask His forgiveness through repentance.

Repentance is first and foremost. Webster defines repentance as the relinquishment of any practice from the conviction that it has offended God.[33] We generally know right from wrong because our pure conscience alerts us to the difference. Our choice after conviction then determines future action. Too many of us make wrong choices to achieve instant gratification, after which often comes a repetition of meaningless surface behaviorism which glazes the offense instead of deep repentance. Webster asserts that real penitence is sorrow or deep contrition for sin as an offense and dishonor to God, a violation of His holy law, and the basest ingratitude towards a Being of infinite benevolence. This concept, called evangelical repentance, is accompanied and followed by amendment of life.

Matthew 3:2 records John the Baptist saying, *"Repent, for the kingdom of heaven is at hand!"* The Baptist is imploring everyone who has offended God through sin to ask His forgiveness for the past in order to move on with their lives clothed in the forgiving righteousness of God. After John had been imprisoned for preaching the Good News of the kingdom through repentance, Jesus comes into town. He begins to preach, *"Repent, for the kingdom of heaven is at hand" (Matthew 4:17)*. Notice, He doesn't say, "Believe in Me." Although believing Him is a vital key to leading a successful life, His first teaching was to repent. Until you recognize that you are wrong in your sins, you will find no shelter in the gospel. You must first surrender the control sin has on your life and allow God to govern you into a life of holiness.

Repentance is so vitally important that Jesus continued the message after John's arrest denied him the opportunity for further teaching of the gospel! In Luke 13:3, 5, Jesus says, *"Unless you repent you will...perish."* Repentance leads to salvation, freedom, and restoration from sin darkness. *"For godly sorrow produces repentance to salvation not to be regretted; but the sorrow of the world produces death" (2 Corinthians 7:10)*. Sincere and genuine remorse for your sins will usher in showers of forgiveness, cleansing you of the crimson stains of a life in sin. 2 Peter 3:9 tells us that *"the Lord is not slack concerning His promise, as some count slackness, but longsuffering toward us, not willing that any should perish but that all should come to repentance."*

Luke records in the book of Acts that all who took Jesus at His word to preach the Good News of the gospel first demanded repentance.

> *Therefore, since we are the offspring of God, we ought not to think that the Divine Nature is like gold or silver or stone, something shaped by art and man's devising. Truly, these times of ignorance God overlooked, but now commands all men everywhere to repent.*
> *Acts 17:29-30*

Whatever your initial thoughts and concepts of God are, He sets them aside, realizing that you are susceptible to other influences when you are not spiritually aware and tuned in to Him. Hence, He insists that you repent to access His eternal protection. *"Repent therefore and be converted, that your sins may be blotted out"* (Acts 3:19). In order for your life to be turned around to pursue holiness, you MUST first repent!

Then Peter said to them, *"Repent, and let every one of you be baptized in the name of Jesus Christ for the remission of sins"* (Acts 2:38). God loves us all the same. However, He has an enthusiastic interest over any one sinner that opens his or her heart to receive His undying love! *"I say to you that likewise there will be more joy over one sinner who repents than over ninety-nine just persons who need no repentance"* (Luke 15:7).

Salvation

Salvation comes only by the works Jesus perfected on the cross of Calvary. Salvation eradicates sin. When man sinned in the Garden, his condemnation created an eternal separation from God. However, God created man for eternal relationship, and separation was not a part of His divine creation. The separation of man from God because of sin temporarily altered God's initial plan. Through His sovereignty, He provided a solution to man's lack of obedience. Jesus became the only provision whereby man became whole or right with God after the fall of his sin nature. Jesus is the answer!

John 3:3 states, *"Jesus answered and said to him, Most assuredly, I say to you, unless one is born again, he cannot see the kingdom of God."* Here in the Scripture we find a mandate from the Creator, a must for salvation. We were born into a sinful world through the sinful, flesh nature of man. A physical birth cannot produce a spiritual being.

Jesus' birth was not of the order of the flesh, although He was born of woman. Mary conceived of the Holy Spirit without physical contact with man. Hence, God incarnate entered the world via the spiritual likeness of a natural process that He perfected which could never be challenged.

We must be born again because of disobedience. The flesh of a man will never willingly cooperate with the spirit of a man. The flesh always falls short of anything it attempts to offer a spiritual process. *"For all have sinned and fall short of the glory of God" (Romans 3:23).* Here we find the reason why salvation is necessary for man. Our flesh will block any spiritual progress we are to experience, because it loves sin. The things produced from the flesh are fleshly; the things originated from the spirit are spiritual. Sin does not originate from the spirit; it is a byproduct of the flesh nature of man. Again, Tennyson's *In Memoriam* identifies our numbered days on earth and accountability:

> My own dim life should teach me this,
> That life shall live for evermore,
> Else earth is darkness at the core,
> And dust and ashes all that is.[34]

The poet is very careful to highlight that humanity is predetermined but that man's spirit life (soul) itself is eternal. God holds us accountable for our spiritual and moral conduct, which we exhibit through our physical body. Notice, the soul is everlasting, while the physical body will return to dust and ashes. At the end of the line, we decide to spend eternity either with or without God.

We have but one way to become saved, born-again, or regenerated. *"If you confess with your mouth the Lord Jesus and believe in your heart that God raised Him from the dead, you will be saved" (Romans 10:9).* Here we see the only way by which salvation will come. This process is plain and simple, but it does require an act of will over your fleshly desire. Your flesh will insist that this process is an unnecessary farce. *"But the natural man does not receive the things of the Spirit of God, for they are foolishness to him; nor can he know them because they are spiritually discerned" (1 Corinthians 2:14).* The void or emptiness that you experience in sin is the result of refusing salvation to flow in your life. When you receive this gift from God, you will experience the lifting of a heavy burden from your shoulders and a glow beyond anything you have ever experienced in your life. *"Therefore if the Son makes you free, you shall be free indeed" (John 8:54).*

If you believe that Jesus is the Christ, and the Savior of the world who gave His life to save you from eternal separation from God Almighty, and is willing to help you live for Him; pray this prayer with me:

> Dear God, I need you in my life. My sin and shame has put distance between us. I know that eternal death is the deserving outcome for my unacceptable life choices. Jesus, I confess You as my personal Savior, I believe in my heart that Your crucified death washed me clean purchasing my freedom from sin and shame. Your resurrection gives me a fresh start in You. Now, I invite Your spirit into my life to change me and help me make life choices that Glorify you. Thank You Lord for saving me, Amen!

Please write us and share your salvation experience. (Valiant Living Christian Center, P.O. Box 1164, Kent, WA 98035)

Chapter 17

Holy Spirit
Come Live in Me

God is a good and gracious God. As we grow in our relationship with Him, we find that giving gifts is a high-priority love language of His. God gave His only begotten Son as a sacrificial offering for our sins. The gift was free and without prerequisites. In fact, we were at our worst when this precious gift came to us. Just as God afforded us the freedom to choose the gift of salvation, He extends us the same freedom when we receive the infilling of the Holy Spirit. Salvation is a precursor to experiencing the active and powerful presence of the Holy Spirit in our lives.

The Lord never intended for us to be alone. He showed us how to walk in relationship with God and how to live an effective life to influence good in others by meeting their needs. We will endure times of challenge, but even in those times, He has promised to be with us. *"The Helper, the Holy Spirit, whom the Father will send in My name, He will teach you all things, and bring to your remembrance all things that I said to you" (John 14:26).* After showing us a good faith walk, Jesus knew He had to return to the throne to occupy His seat at the right hand of God. The Holy Spirit was the fulfillment of His promise to provide help for us to glorify Him.

The Holy Spirit is the unlimited source of power that materializes our faith walk. Acts 1:8 declares, *"You shall receive power when the Holy Spirit has come upon you; and you shall be witnesses to me in Jerusalem, and in all Judea and Samaria, and to the end of the earth."* As you work out your own soul's salvation, you acquire opportunities to participate in leading others to salvation. Being the answer to someone else's petition of God requires boldness. Most of us do not have this type of boldness. The Holy Spirit is the agent that leads us into bold action. In order to receive Him, you have to ask Him to fill you.

God wants you to have every gift that He has for you. You must believe that this provision is His will for your life. *"If you then, being evil, know how to give good gifts to your children, how much more will your Father give the Holy Spirit to those who ask Him?" (Luke 11:13).* We cannot beat God at giving. We cannot give Him anything to equal or surpass all that He has given us. Just receive, and go in the power of His might to spread the Good News of the gospel. God has everything that we need. Just receive. We're like a child receiving a gift at Christmas that he had asked of his parent. The child asked in faith, believing that he would get his gift, and he acted as though he had it before he ever physically saw or touched it in his hands. If we could only teach ourselves to come to the Lord as children do!

The gift of the infilling is for all who are saved and will receive it. Acts 2:4 illustrates, *"They were all filled with the Holy Spirit and began to speak with other tongues, as the Spirit gave them utterance."* What is utterance? Utterance is going beyond the limits of natural understanding. Let me introduce 1 Corinthians 14:2, *"For he who speaks in a tongue does not speak to men but to God, for no one understands him; however, in the spirit he speaks mysteries."* If no one understands you and you speak mysteries, you are uttering. Do not be intimidated by not being able to explain what you are experiencing. You are experiencing the supernatural power of the Holy Spirit. If you desire to understand or interpret what you are uttering, ask God. In order to benefit from this experience, you must operate in full faith, overriding all sense-knowledge signals of acceptance or rejection from yourself and others. You are in a Holy Spirit moment. Swim through it, and enjoy it! Praise God!

You can pray in your prayer language and not understand what you are praying because it is a mystery, according to 1 Corinthians 14:14-15. However, you can also pray and sing with the spirit (prayer language) and/or you can pray and sing with understanding (your native language). I suggest that you do both. God hears everything as you release this special offering from your heart and soul.

God did not limit this infilling to two, three, or even a few of the disciples. Acts 2:4 speaks of all. They all were filled with the Holy Spirit! If you desire to receive from God, then He has already given to you. Just thank Him, and receive the gift! Acts 2:39 authenticates, *"For the promise is to you and to your children, and to all who are afar off, as many as the Lord our God will call."* You have no reason why your infilling, as that of the disciples on the day of Pentecost, should not happen. Today is the day for you. This hour is your hour, right here, right now. Open your mouth, and begin to speak boldly as the Spirit gives you utterance. Receive the infilling of the Holy Spirit!

If you have accepted Jesus as your Lord and Savior and believe that the infilling of the Holy Spirit is a free gift to you from God; pray this prayer with me and receive it:

Father God, I come to you in the name of Jesus believing, by faith, that it is your pleasure to give good things to me. According to your promise, I ask you to fill me with the Holy Spirit. I thank you for filling me and I receive You, Holy

Spirit, with joy and gratitude in my heart. I can now speak in tongues. Amen!

Now pray without ceasing in your new heavenly language and write us to share your new experience. (Valiant Living Christian Center, P.O. Box 1164, Kent, WA 98035)

Conclusion

The totality of this work considered several stages and aspects of man's lifespan that contribute to his past, current, and future relationship with God while searching for the answer to the question asked within the title: Do you have what it takes to live valiantly? Each part within this work addresses key factors to help uncover the answer to the specific focus of this book: why does man struggle to develop and maintain a significant relationship with God?

Repentance is the spiritual key to unlock the kingdom of heaven for the unbeliever. The acceptance of a new spiritual birth led by the Spirit of God is paramount to all other factors within this study. Helping man to understand his divine origin, authority, and created purpose is the focal point. Man was created to fellowship with God intimately through a free and transparent spiritual union.

Worship is another key to establishing and sustaining this delicate and essential dialogue. After opening this channel of communication, man must then focus on his ordained authority to take dominion over the earth and to prepare for eternal existence. Once man understands who he is and to whom he belongs, his next transition is to cross over spiritually into the supernatural while perfecting self-control of his physical body. Suppressing his flesh while operating from his spirit will draw him toward God, causing him to reach out to others and to open their awareness to their rightful place in God.

By allowing the will of God to work consistently in his life, man will come to know and understand the desires of his Creator. Obtaining clear, revolutionary wisdom from his Maker will result in ready obedience. However, man does have the office of volition to do as he wishes. Here is where the intensity increases, because man can choose to exercise the will of flesh over the spirit. The whole of man consists of spirit, soul, and body, with the soul as the pivotal point. Here a man makes a decision under the influence of the spirit to obey or the flesh to disobey. Whenever man creates a barrier to ignore the Almighty, man suffers. Pressing into the presence of God with a right heart from a spirit of humility serves to synchronize our spirit to His. Such synchronization leads man personally to honor and respect the Father's sacrifice to regenerate his life anew. Now man can enjoy the goodness of God as joint heir with Christ. God brings all of heaven's resources to uphold his every need.

Finally, this work illustrates the importance of distinguishing who God made man to be while discovering his created purpose, understanding his divine origin and authority, defining how to fulfill God's plan for his life, and determining how to get that plan done. God designed us to live valiant lives passionately focused on our Creator first, others next, and then ourselves. Anything less creates a struggle in life. This struggle confirms that consistently enabling and encouraging others to develop a significant heart relationship with God is quintessential. Each one who cultivates a sustained relationship with the Almighty would aggregately contribute to changing the fabric of our world. Furthermore, this cumulative change would discourage mankind from dastardly clinging to sin as salvation from holiness. You have what you need. Use what God gave you to discover and fulfill your God-given assignment!

Bill Blake is Founding Pastor of Valiant Living Christian Center in Kent, Washington.

He resigned at the pinnacle of his career after 23 years of excellent government service from Executive Service to answer the call to full-time ministry. He has already spent two decades motivating and inspiring others to use their God-given abilities to have Kingdom impact.

He is a veteran of the United States Marine Corps with extensive international travel experience. Throughout his career he has lived on three continents and traveled over five while providing protection for a host of foreign and domestic dignitaries.

Bill Blake resides in the Kent area with his wife, Davina and their children.

To learn more about teachings that are available by Bill Blake, write to:

**Bill Blake
P.O. Box 1164
Kent, WA 98035**

Please include your prayer requests and comments when you write.

End Notes

1. *Webster's II New Riverside University Dictionary*, 2nd ed., s.v. "Valiant."
2. Grape, John T., "Jesus Paid It All," lyrics by Hall, Elvina M., in *The New Church Hymnal*, Jacque Anderson, ed. (Newbury Park, CA: Lexicon Music, 1976).
3. Altrogge, Mark, music and lyrics, "I Stand in Awe of You" (Nashville, TN: Mercy Publishing, 1987).
4. Syverson, Jeff, "Tozer, Aiden Wilson. A 20th Century Prophet (1897 – 1963)," March 6, 2009, http://www.pastorjeff.com/Tozer.html.
5. Winans, Vickie, "To God Be the Glory," lyrics by Crouch, Andre (Detroit, MI: Destiny Joy Publishing and CGI Records, Inc., 1997).
6. Wiley, Fletch, music and lyrics, "Lift High the Lord Our Banner" (Nashville, TN: World Music, 1993).
7. Houston, Joel, music and lyrics, "I'll Stand, Arms Wide, Heart Abandoned" (Sydney, Australia: Hillsong, 2006).
8. Third Day, music and lyrics, "Just to Be with You," christianlyricsonline.com, March 6, 2009, http://www.christianlyricsonline.com/artists/third-day/love-song.html.

9. "When the student is ready, the teacher will appear," thinkexist.com, March 7, 2009, http://en.thinkexist.com/search/searchQuotation.asp?search=%93When+the+student+is+ready%2C+the+teacher+appears.%94++.
10. Browning, Robert, "Andrea Del Sarto," line 97.
11. Tom Weir, "Racetrack was Borel's classroom," *USA Today*, May 18, 2007.
12. *Webster's II New Riverside University Dictionary*, 2nd ed., s.v. "Prisoner."
13. Harmon, Nancy, music and lyrics, "My Soul Has Escaped" (Detroit, MI: Love Special Products Music and CGI Records, Inc., 1997).
14. *Webster's II New Riverside University Dictionary*, 2nd ed., s.v. "Bondservant."
15. Runyan, William M., "Great is Thy Faithfulness," lyrics by Chisholm, T. O., in *The New Church Hymnal*.
16. Mullens, Rich, music and lyrics, "Our God Is an Awesome God" (Nashville, TN: Reunion Records, 1988).
17. King, Kerrith H., "The Water Pump Story," Anectdotes, March 7, 2009, http://www.comcom121.org/anecdote.htm#pump.
18. Graafsma, Debbye, music and lyrics, "Mighty Warrior" (Mobile, AL: Integrity Music/ASCAP, 1983).
19. Wesolek, Kim, music and lyrics, "You Alone" (Seattle, WA: Christian Faith Center, 1999).
20. Donne, John, Meditation XVII.
21. "John Donne" < http://isu.indstate.edu/ilnprof/ENG451/ISLAND/>
22. Warner, Daniel S., music and lyrics, "Child of The King" (public domain).

23. Tennyson, Alfred, In Memoriam, canto 27, lines 13-16.
24. Jones, Linda Sutton, "Racial Slur," Jose Pino, March 7, 2009, http://josepino.com/humor/?racial.jpc.
25. Markham, Edwin, quotesandpoem.com, March 6, 2009, http://www.quotesandpoem.com/quotes/show-quotes/author/edwin_markham/115803.
26. Sewell, Hampton H., "He Included Me," lyrics by Oatman, Johnson Jr. (public domain).
27. Marx, Karl, "From each according to his ability, to each according to his need," Wikipedia, March 7, 2009, http://en.wikipedia.org/wiki/From_each_according_to_his_ability,_to_each_according_to_his_need.
28. Maxey, Duane V., "The Story of 'The Curfew Must Not Ring Tonight,'" 30 Nov 2008, <http://wesley.nnu.edu/wesleyctr/books/2001-2100/HDM2007.PDF>.
29. Thorpe, Rose Hartwick, "Curfew Must Not Ring Tonight," March 6, 2009, http://womenshistory.about.com/library/etext/poem1/blp_thorpe_curfew.htm
30. Montgomery, Frank and Monthy, Bruce, music and lyrics, "Your Name in All the Earth" (Seattle, WA: Christian Faith Center, 1999).
31. Ron Kenoly, music and lyrics, "Jesus Is Alive" (Mobile, AL: Integrity Music/ASCAP, 1987).
32. Carlyle, Thomas, Sartor Resartus, chapter 3, line 17.
33. Webster's 1828 Dictionary Online, s.v. "Repent," November 29, 2008, <http://1828.mshaffer.com/d/search/word,repent>.
34. Tennyson, Alfred, In Memoriam, canto 34, lines 1-4.

Printed in the United States
146036LV00001B/3/P